The New Paradigm for
Financial Markets

The Age of Fallibility: The Consequences of the War on Terror

The Bubble of American Supremacy: The Cost of Bush's War in Iraq

George Soros on Globalization

Open Society: Reforming Global Capitalism

The Crisis of Global Capitalism: Open Society Endangered

Soros on Soros: Staying Ahead of the Curve

Underwriting Democracy

Opening the Soviet System

The Alchemy of Finance: Reading the Mind of the Market

GEORGE SOROS

The New Paradigm for Financial Markets

THE CREDIT CRISIS OF 2008 AND WHAT IT MEANS

PublicAffairs

NEW YORK

No part of this book may be reproduced in any manner whatsoever without written permission except in the case of brief quotations embodied in critical articles and reviews. For information, address PublicAffairs, 250 West 57th Street, Suite 1321, New York, NY 10107. PublicAffairs books are available at special discounts for bulk purchases in the U.S. by corporations, institutions, and other organizations. For more information, please contact the Special Markets Department at the Perseus Books Group, 2300 Chestnut Street, Suite 200, Philadelphia, PA 19103, call (800) 810-4145, x5000, or email special.markets@perseusbooks.com.

TEXT SET IN JANSON TEXT

Cataloging-in-Publication Data is available from the Library of Congress.
ISBN 978-1-58648-683-9 (hardback)
ISBN 978-1-58648-684-6 (e-book)

FIRST EDITION

1 3 5 7 9 10 8 6 4 2

Contents

Introduction

We are in the midst of the worst financial crisis since the 1930s. In some ways it resembles other crises that have occurred in the last twenty-five years, but there is a profound difference: the current crisis marks the end of an era of credit expansion based on the dollar as the international reserve currency. The periodic crises were part of a larger boom-bust process; the current crisis is the culmination of a super-boom that has lasted for more than twenty-five years.

To understand what is going on we need a new paradigm. The currently prevailing paradigm, namely that financial markets tend towards equilibrium, is both false and misleading; our current troubles can be largely attributed to the fact that the international financial system has been developed on the basis of that paradigm.

The new paradigm I am proposing is not confined to the financial markets. It deals with the relationship between thinking and reality, and it claims that misconceptions and misinterpretations play a major role in shaping the course of history. I started developing this conceptual framework as a student at the London School of Economics before I became active in the financial markets. As I have written before, I was greatly influenced by the philosophy of Karl Popper, and this made me question the assumptions on which the theory of perfect competition is based, in particular the assumption of perfect knowledge. I came to realize that market participants cannot base their decisions on knowledge alone, and their biased perceptions have ways of influencing not only market prices but also the fundamentals that those prices are supposed to reflect. I argued that the participants' thinking plays a dual function. On the one hand, they seek to understand their situation. I called this the cognitive function. On the other hand, they try to change the situation. I called this the participating or manipulative function. The two functions work in opposite directions and, under certain circumstances, they can interfere with each other. I called this interference reflexivity.

When I became a market participant, I applied my conceptual framework to the financial markets. It allowed me to gain a better understanding of initially self-reinforcing but eventually self-defeating boom-bust processes, and I put that insight to good use as the manager of a hedge fund. I expounded the theory of reflexivity in my first book, *The Alchemy of Finance*, which was published in 1987. The book acquired a cult following, but the theory of reflexivity was not taken seriously in academic circles. I myself harbored grave doubts about whether I was saying something new and significant. After all, I was dealing with one of the most basic and most thoroughly studied problems of philosophy, and everything that could be said on the subject had probably already been said. Nevertheless, my conceptual framework remained something very important for me personally. It guided me both in making money as a hedge fund manager and in spending it as a philanthropist, and it became an integral part of my identity.

When the financial crisis erupted, I had retired from actively managing my fund, having previously changed its status from an aggressive hedge fund to a more sedate endowment fund. The crisis forced me, however, to refocus my attention on the financial markets, and I became more actively engaged in making investment decisions. Then, towards the end of 2007, I decided to write a book analyzing and explaining the current situation. I was motivated by three considerations. First, a new paradigm was urgently needed for a better understanding of what is going on. Second, engaging in a serious study could help me in my investment decisions. Third, by providing a timely insight into the financial markets, I would ensure that the theory of reflexivity would finally receive serious consideration. It is difficult to gain attention for an abstract theory, but people are intensely interested in the financial markets, especially when they are in turmoil. I have already used the financial markets as a laboratory for testing the theory of reflexivity in *The Alchemy of Finance*; the current situation provides an excellent opportunity to demonstrate its relevance and importance. Of the three considerations, the third weighed most heavily in my decision to publish this book.

The fact that I had more than one objective in writing it makes the book more complicated than it would be if it were focused solely on the unfolding financial crisis. Let me explain briefly how the theory of reflexivity applies to the crisis. Contrary to classical economic theory, which assumes perfect knowledge, neither market participants nor the monetary and fiscal authorities can base their decisions purely on knowledge. Their misjudgments and misconceptions affect market prices, and, more importantly, market prices affect the so-called fundamentals that they are supposed to reflect. Market prices do not deviate from a theoretical equilibrium in a random manner, as the current paradigm holds. Participants' and regulators' views never correspond to the actual state of affairs; that is to say, markets never reach the equilibrium postulated by economic theory. There is a two-way reflexive connection between perception and reality which can give rise to initially self-reinforcing but eventually self-defeating boom-bust processes, or bubbles. Every bubble consists of a trend and a misconception that interact in a reflexive manner. There has been a bubble in the U.S. housing market, but the current crisis is not merely the bursting of the housing bubble. It is bigger than the periodic financial crises we have experienced in our lifetime. All those crises are part of what I call a super-bubble—a long-term reflexive process which has evolved over the last twenty-five years or so. It consists of a prevailing trend, credit expansion, and a prevailing misconception, market fundamentalism (aka *laissez-faire* in the nineteenth century), which holds that markets should be given free rein. The previous crises served as successful tests which reinforced the prevailing trend and the prevailing misconception. The current crisis constitutes the turning point when both the trend and the misconception have become unsustainable.

All this needs a lot more explanation. After setting the stage, I devote the first part of this book to the theory of reflexivity, which goes well beyond the financial markets. People interested solely in the current crisis will find it hard going, but those who make the effort will, I hope, find it rewarding. It constitutes my main interest, my life's work. Readers of my previous books will note that I have repeated

some passages from them because the points I am making remain the same. Part 2 draws both on the conceptual framework and on my practical experience as a hedge fund
manager to illuminate the current situation.

Setting the Stage

The outbreak of the current financial crisis can be officially fixed as August 2007. That was when the central banks had to intervene to provide liquidity to the banking system. As the BBC reported:*

- On August 6, American Home Mortgage, one of the largest U.S. independent home loan providers, filed for bankruptcy after laying off the majority of its staff. The company said it was a victim of the slump in the U.S. housing market that had caught out many subprime borrowers and lenders.
- On August 9, short-term credit markets froze up after a large French bank, BNP Paribas, suspended three of its investment funds worth 2 billion euros, citing problems in the U.S. subprime mortgage sector. BNP said it could not value the assets in the funds because the market had disappeared. The European Central Bank pumped 95 billion euros into the eurozone banking system to ease the subprime credit crunch. The U.S. Federal Reserve and the Bank of Japan took similar steps.

*BBC News, "Timeline: Sub-Prime losses: How Did the Sub-Prime Crisis Unfold?" http://news.bbc.co.uk/1/hi/business/7096845.stm.

- On August 10, the European Central Bank provided an extra 61 billion euros of funds for banks. The U.S. Federal Reserve said it would provide as much overnight money as would be needed to combat the credit crunch.

- On August 13, the European Central Bank pumped 47.7 billion euros into the money markets, its third cash injection in as many working days. Central banks in the United States and Japan also topped up earlier injections. Goldman Sachs said it would pump 3 billion dollars into a hedge fund hit by the credit crunch to shore up its value.

- On August 16, Countrywide Financial, the largest U.S. mortgage originator, drew down its entire 11.5 billion dollar credit line. Australian mortgage lender Rams also admitted liquidity problems.

- On August 17, the U.S. Federal Reserve cut the discount rate (the interest rate at which it lends to banks) by a half a percentage point to help banks deal with credit problems. (But it did not help. Subsequently the central banks of the developed world ended up injecting funds on a larger scale for longer periods and accepting a wider range of securities as collateral than ever before in history.)

- On September 13, it was disclosed that Northern Rock (the largest British mortgage banker) was bordering on insolvency (which triggered an old-fashioned bank run—for the first time in Britain in a hundred years).

The crisis was slow in coming, but it could have been anticipated several years in advance. It had its origins in the bursting of the Internet bubble in late 2000. The Fed responded by cutting the federal funds rate from 6.5 percent to

3.5 percent within the space of just a few months. Then came the terrorist attack of September 11, 2001. To counteract the disruption of the economy, the Fed continued to lower rates—all the way down to 1 percent by July 2003, the lowest rate in half a century, where it stayed for a full year. For thirty-one consecutive months the base inflation-adjusted short-term interest rate was negative.

Cheap money engendered a housing bubble, an explosion of leveraged buyouts, and other excesses. When money is free, the rational lender will keep on lending until there is no one else to lend to. Mortgage lenders relaxed their standards and invented new ways to stimulate business and generate fees. Investment banks on Wall Street developed a variety of new techniques to hive credit risk off to other investors, like pension funds and mutual funds, which were hungry for yield. They also created structured investment vehicles (SIVs) to keep their own positions off their balance sheets.

From 2000 until mid-2005, the market value of existing homes grew by more than 50 percent, and there was a frenzy of new construction. Merrill Lynch estimated that about half of all American GDP growth in the first half of 2005 was housing related, either directly, through home building and housing-related purchases like new furniture, or indirectly, by spending the cash generated from the refinancing of mortgages. Martin Feldstein, a former chairman of the Council of Economic Advisers, estimated that from 1997 through 2006, consumers drew more than $9 trillion in cash out of their home equity. A 2005 study led by Alan Greenspan estimated that in the 2000s, home equity withdrawals were financing 3 percent of all personal consumption. By the first quarter of 2006, home equity extraction made up nearly 10 percent of disposable personal income.*

Double-digit price increases in house prices engendered speculation. When the value of property is expected to rise more than the cost of borrowing, it makes sense to own more property than one wants to occupy. By 2005, 40 percent of all homes purchased were not meant to serve as permanent residences but as investments or second homes.† Since growth in real median income was anemic in the 2000s, lenders strained ingenuity to make houses appear affordable. The most popular devices were adjustable rate mortgages (ARMs) with "teaser," below-market initial rates for an initial two-year period. It was assumed that after two years, when the higher rate kicked in, the mortgage would be refinanced, taking advantage of the higher prices and generating a new set of fees for the lenders. Credit standards collapsed, and mortgages were made widely available to people with low credit ratings (called subprime mortgages), many of whom were well-to-do. "Alt-A" (or liar loans), with low or no documentation, were common, including, at the extreme, "ninja" loans (no job, no income, no assets), frequently with the active connivance of the mortgage brokers and mortgage lenders.

*_Economist_, September 10, 2005; Martin Feldstein, "Housing, Credit Markets and the Business Cycle," National Bureau of Economic Research working paper 13,471, October 2007; Alan Greenspan and James Kennedy, "Estimates of Home Mortgage Origination, Repayments, and Debts on One- to Four-Family Residences," Federal Reserve staff working paper 2005–41 (data updated through 2007 by Dr. Kennedy and furnished to the author).

†Joseph R. Mason and Joshua Rosner, "How Resilient Are Mortgage Backed Securities to Collateralized Debt Obligation Market Disruption?" paper presented at the Hudson Institute, Washington, D.C., February 15, 2007, 11.

Banks sold off their riskiest mortgages by repackaging them into securities called collateralized debt obligations (CDOs). CDOs channeled the cash flows from thousands of mortgages into a series of tiered, or tranched, bonds with risks and yields tuned to different investor tastes. The top-tier tranches, which comprised perhaps 80 percent of the bonds, would have first call on all underlying cash flows, so they could be sold with a AAA rating. The lower tiers absorbed first-dollar risks but carried higher yields. In practice, the bankers and the rating agencies grossly underestimated the risks inherent in absurdities like ninja loans.

Securitization was meant to reduce risks through risk tiering and geographic diversification. As it turned out, they increased the risks by transferring ownership of mortgages from bankers who knew their customers to investors who did not. Instead of a bank or savings and loan approving a credit and retaining it on its books, loans were sourced by brokers; temporarily "'warehoused" by thinly capitalized "mortgage bankers"; then sold en bloc to investment banks, who manufactured the CDOs, which were rated by ratings agencies and sold off to institutional investors. All income from the original sourcing through the final placement was fee based—the higher the volumes, the bigger the bonuses. The prospect of earning fees without incurring risks encouraged lax and deceptive business practices. The subprime area, which dealt with inexperienced and uninformed customers, was rife with fraudulent activities. The word "teaser rates" gave the game away.

Starting around 2005, securitization became a mania. It was easy and fast to create "synthetic" securities that mimicked the risks of real securities but did not carry the expense of buying and assembling actual loans. Risky paper could therefore be multiplied well beyond the actual supply in the market. Enterprising investment bankers sliced up CDOs and repackaged them into CDOs of CDOs, or CDO^{2}s. There were even CDO^{3}s. The highest slices of lower-rated CDOs obtained AAA ratings. In this way more AAA liabilities were created than there were AAA assets. Towards the end, synthetic products accounted for more than half the trading volume.

The securitization mania was not confined to mortgages and spread to other forms of credit. By far the largest synthetic market is constituted by credit default swaps (CDSs). This arcane synthetic financial instrument was invented in Europe in the early 1990s. Early CDSs were customized agreements between two banks. Bank A, the swap seller (protection purchaser), agreed to pay an annual fee for a set period of years to Bank B, the swap buyer (protection seller), with respect to a specific portfolio of loans. Bank B would commit to making good Bank A's losses on portfolio defaults during the life of the swap. Prior to CDSs, a bank wishing to diversify its portfolio would need to buy or sell pieces of loans, which was complicated because it required the permission of the borrower; consequently, this form of diversification became very popular. Terms were standardized, and the notional value of the contracts grew to about a trillion dollars by 2000.

Hedge funds entered the market in force in the early 2000s. Specialized credit hedge funds effectively acted as unlicensed insurance companies, collecting premiums on the CDOs and other securities that they insured. The value of the insurance was often questionable because contracts could be assigned without notifying the counterparties. The market grew exponentially until it came to overshadow all other markets in nominal terms. The estimated nominal value of CDS contracts outstanding is $42.6 trillion. To put matters in perspective, this is equal to almost the entire household wealth of the United States. The capitalization of the U.S. stock market is $18.5 trillion, and the U.S. treasuries market is only $4.5 trillion.

The securitization mania led to an enormous increase in the use of leverage. To hold ordinary bonds requires a margin of 10 percent; synthetic bonds created by credit default swaps can be traded on a margin of 1.5 percent. This allowed hedge funds to show good profits by exploiting risk differentials on a leveraged basis, driving down risk premiums.

It was bound to end badly. There was a precedent to go by. The market in collateralized mortgage obligations (CMOs) started to develop in the 1980s. In 1994, the market in the lowest-rated tranches—or "toxic waste," as they were known—blew up when a $2 billion hedge fund could not meet a margin call, leading to the demise of Kidder Peabody and total losses of about $55 billion. But no regulatory action was taken. Former Federal Reserve governor Edward M. Gramlich privately warned Federal Reserve Chairman Alan Greenspan about abusive behavior in the subprime mortgage markets in 2000, but the warning was swept aside. Gramlich went public with his worries in 2007 and published a book on the subprime bubble just before the crisis first broke. Charles Kindleberger, an expert on bubbles, warned of the housing bubble in 2002. Martin Feldstein, Paul Volcker (former chairman of the Federal Reserve), and Bill Rhodes (a senior official of Citibank) all made bearish warnings. Nouriel Roubini predicted that the housing bubble would lead to a recession in 2006. But no one, including myself, anticipated how big the bubble could grow and how long it could last. As the *Wall Street Journal* recently noted, there were many hedge funds taking a bearish stance on housing, but "they suffered such painful losses waiting for a collapse" that most eventually gave up their positions.*

Signs of trouble started to multiply early in 2007. On February 22, HSBC fired the head of its U.S. mortgage lending business, recognizing losses reaching $10.8 billion. On March 9, DR Horton, the biggest U.S. homebuilder, warned of losses from subprime mortgages. On March 12, New Century Financial, one of the biggest subprime lenders, had its shares suspended from trading amid fears that the company was headed for bankruptcy. On March 13, it was reported that late payments on mortgages and home foreclosures rose to new highs. On March 16, Accredited Home Lenders Holding put up $2.7 billion of its subprime loan book for sale at a heavy discount to generate cash for business operations. On April 2, New Century Financial filed for Chapter 11 bankruptcy protection after it was forced to repurchase billions of dollars worth of bad loans.†

On June 15, 2007, Bear Stearns announced that two large mortgage hedge funds were having trouble meeting margin calls. Bear grudgingly created a $3.2 billion credit line to bail out one fund and let the other collapse. Investors' equity of $1.5 billion was mostly wiped out.

Wall Street Journal, February 27, 2008, and January 15, 2008; *New York Times*, October 26, 2007.

†"Bleak Housing Outlook for US Firm," *BBC News*, March 8, 2007, http://news.bbc.co.uk/2/hi/business/6429815.stm.

The failure of the two Bear Stearns mortgage hedge funds in June badly rattled the markets, but U.S. Federal Reserve Chairman Ben Bernanke and other senior officials reassured the public that the subprime problem was an isolated phenomenon. Prices stabilized, although the flow of bad news continued unabated. As late as July 20, Bernanke still estimated subprime losses at only about $100 billion. When Merrill Lynch and Citigroup took big write-downs on in-house collateralized debt obligations, the markets actually staged a relief rally. The S&P 500 hit a new high in mid-July.

It was only at the beginning of August that financial markets really took fright. It came as a shock when Bear Stearns filed for bankruptcy protection for two hedge funds exposed to subprime loans and stopped clients from withdrawing cash from a third fund. As mentioned, Bear Stearns had tried to save these entities by providing $3.2 billion of additional funding.

Once the crisis erupted, financial markets unraveled with remarkable rapidity. Everything that could go wrong did. A surprisingly large number of weaknesses were revealed in a remarkably short period of time. What started with low-grade subprime mortgages soon spread to CDOs, particularly those synthetic ones that were constructed out of the top slice of subprime mortgages. The CDOs themselves were not readily tradable, but there were tradable indexes representing the various branches. Investors looking for cover and short sellers looking for profits rushed to sell these indexes, and they declined precipitously, bringing the value of the various branches of CDOs that they were supposed to represent into question. Investment banks carried large positions of CDOs off balance sheet in so-called structured investment vehicles

(SIVs). The SIVs financed their positions by issuing asset-backed commercial paper. As the value of CDOs came into question, the asset-backed commercial paper market dried up, and the investment banks were forced to bail out their SIVs. Most investment banks took the SIVs into their balance sheets and were forced to recognize large losses in the process. Investment banks were also sitting on large loan commitments to finance leveraged buyouts. In the normal course of events, they would package these loans as collateralized loan obligations (CLOs) and sell them off, but the CLO market came to a standstill together with the CDO market, and the banks were left holding a bag worth about $250 billion. Some banks allowed their SIVs to go bust, and some reneged on their leveraged buyout obligations. This, together with the size of the losses incurred by the banks, served to unnerve the stock market, and price movements became chaotic. So-called market-neutral hedge funds, which exploit small discrepancies in market prices by using very high leverage, ceased to be market neutral and incurred unusual losses. A few highly leveraged ones were wiped out, damaging the reputation of their sponsors and unleashing lawsuits.

All this put tremendous pressure on the banking system. Banks had to put additional items on their balance sheets at a time when their capital base was impaired by unexpected losses. They had difficulty assessing their exposure and even greater difficulties estimating the exposure of their counterparts. Consequently they were reluctant to lend to each other and eager to hoard their liquidity. At first, central banks found it difficult to inject enough liquidity because commercial banks avoided using any of the facilities which had an onus attached to them, and they were also reluctant to deal with each other, but eventually these obstacles were overcome. After all, if there is one thing central banks know how to do, that is to provide liquidity. Only the Bank of England suffered a major debacle when it attempted to rescue Northern Rock, an overextended mortgage lender. Its rescue effort resulted in a run on the bank. Eventually Northern Rock was nationalized and its obligations added to the national debt, pushing the United Kingdom beyond the limits imposed by the Maastricht Treaty.

Although liquidity had been provided, the crisis refused to abate. Credit spreads continued to widen. Almost all the major banks—Citigroup, Merrill Lynch, Lehman Brothers, Bank of America, Wachovia, UBS, Credit Suisse—announced major write-downs in the fourth quarter, and most have signaled continued write-downs in 2008. Both AIG and Credit Suisse made preliminary fourth-quarter write-down announcements that they repeatedly revised, conveying the doubtless accurate impression that they had lost control of their balance sheets. A $7.2 billion trading fiasco at Société Générale announced on January 25, 2008, coincided with a selling climax in the stock market and an extraordinary 75 basis point cut in the federal funds rate eight days before the regularly scheduled meeting, when the rate was cut a further 50 basis points. This was unprecedented.

Distress spread from residential real estate to credit card debt, auto debt, and commercial real estate. Trouble at the monoline insurance companies, which traditionally specialized in municipal bonds but ventured into insuring structured and synthetic products, caused the municipal bond market to be disrupted. An even larger unresolved problem is looming in the credit default swaps market.

Over the past several decades the United States has weathered several major financial crises, like the international lending crisis of the 1980s and the savings and loan crisis of the early 1990s. But the current crisis is of an entirely different character. It has spread from one segment of the market to others, particularly those which employ newly created structured and synthetic instruments. Both the exposure and the capital base of the major financial institutions have been brought into question, and the uncertainties are likely to remain unresolved for an extended period of time. This is impeding the normal functioning of the financial system and is liable to have far-reaching consequences for the real economy.

Both the financial markets and the financial authorities have been very slow to recognize that the real economy is bound to be affected. It is hard to understand why this should be so. The real economy was stimulated by credit expansion. Why should it not be negatively affected by credit contraction? One cannot escape the conclusion that both the financial authorities and market participants harbor fundamental misconceptions about the way financial markets function. These misconceptions have manifested themselves not only in a failure to understand what is going on; they have given rise to the excesses which are at the root of the current market turmoil.

In Part 1, I shall lay out the conceptual framework in terms of which the functioning of financial markets can be understood. In Part 2, I shall apply that framework to the present moment in history.

The New Paradigm for
Financial Markets

PART I

Perspective

CHAPTER 1

The Core Idea

My starting point is that our understanding of the world in which we live is inherently imperfect because we are part of the world we seek to understand. There may be other factors that interfere with our ability to acquire knowledge of the natural world, but the fact that we are part of the world poses a formidable obstacle to the understanding of human affairs.

Understanding a situation and participating in it involves two different functions. On the one hand people seek to understand the world in which they live. I call this the cognitive function. On the other, people seek to make an impact on the world and change it to their advantage. I used to call this the participating function, but now I consider it more appropriate to call it the manipulative function.* If the two functions were isolated from each other they could serve their purpose perfectly well: the participants' understanding could qualify as knowledge, and their actions could have the desired

---

*Cognitive scientists call it the executive function. Aristotle called it practical reason to distinguish it from theoretical reason, which is the equivalent of the cognitive function.

results. For this reason it is tempting to postulate that the functions do in fact operate in isolation. Indeed, that assumption has been made, most notably in economic theory. But the assumption is not justified, except in very exceptional circumstances where the participants make a special effort to keep the two functions separate. That may be the case with social scientists who are single-mindedly devoted to the pursuit of knowledge; but it is not true of the participants in the events that social scientists study. For reasons I shall explore later, social scientists, particularly economists, tend to ignore this fact.

When both functions are in operation at the same time they may interfere with each other. For the cognitive function to produce knowledge it must take social phenomena as independently given; only then will the phenomena qualify as facts to which the observer's statements may correspond. Similarly, decisions need to be based on knowledge to produce the desired results. But when both functions operate simultaneously, the phenomena do not consist only of facts but also of intentions and expectations about the future. The past may be uniquely determined, but the future is contingent on the participants' decisions. Consequently the participants cannot base their decisions on knowledge because they have to deal not only with present and past facts but also with contingencies concerning the future. The role that intentions and expectations about the future play in social situations sets up a two-way connection between the participants' thinking and the situation in which they participate, which has a deleterious effect on both: it introduces an element of contingency or uncertainty into the course of events, and it prevents the participants' views from qualifying as knowledge.

For a function to be uniquely determined, it needs an independent variable which determines the value of the dependent variable. In the cognitive function the actual state of affairs is supposed to be the independent variable, and the participants' views the dependent one; in the manipulative function it is the other way round. In reflexive situations each function deprives the other of the independent variable which it would need to produce determinate results. I have given the two-way interference a name: reflexivity. Reflexive situations are characterized by a *lack of correspondence* between the participants' views and the actual state of affairs. Take the stock market, for example. People buy and sell stocks in anticipation of future stock prices, but those prices are contingent on the investors' expectations. The expectations cannot qualify as knowledge. In the absence of knowledge, participants must introduce an element of judgment or bias into their decision making. As a result, outcomes are liable to diverge from expectations.

Economic theory has gone to great lengths to exclude reflexivity from its subject matter. At first, classical economists simply assumed that market participants base their decisions on perfect knowledge: one of the postulates on which the theory of perfect competition was based was perfect knowledge. Building on those postulates, economists constructed demand curves and supply curves and claimed that those curves governed the participants' decisions. When the construct came under attack, they took refuge behind a methodological convention. Lionel Robbins, who was my professor at the London School of Economics, argued that economics is concerned only with the relationship between demand and supply; what goes into constituting demand and supply is beyond its scope.* By taking demand and supply as independently given he eliminated the possibility that there could be a reflexive interconnection between the two. This approach was later carried to an extreme in rational expectations theory, which somehow contrived to reach the conclusion that future market prices can also be independently determined and are not contingent on the biases and flawed perceptions prevailing among market participants.

I contend that rational expectations theory totally misinterprets how financial markets operate. Although rational expectations theory is no longer taken seriously outside academic circles, the idea that financial markets are self-correcting and tend towards equilibrium remains the prevailing paradigm on which the various synthetic instruments and valuation models which have come to play such a dominant role in financial markets are based. I contend that the prevailing paradigm is false and urgently needs to be replaced.

The fact is that participants cannot base their decisions on knowledge. The two-way, reflexive connection between the cognitive and manipulating functions introduces an element of uncertainty or indeterminacy into both functions. That applies both to market participants and to the financial authorities who are in charge of macro-economic policy and are supposed to supervise and regulate markets. The members of both groups act on the basis of an imperfect understanding of the situation in which they participate. The element of uncertainty inherent in the two-way reflexive

*Lionel Robbins, *An Essay on the Nature and Significance of Economic Science* (London: Macmillan, 1932).

connection between the cognitive and manipulative functions cannot be eliminated; but our understanding, and our ability to cope with the situation, would be greatly improved if we recognized this fact.

This brings me to the central idea in my conceptual framework: I contend that social events have a different structure from natural phenomena. In natural phenomena there is a causal chain that links one set of facts directly with the next. In human affairs the course of events is more complicated. Not only facts are involved but also the participants' views and the interplay between them enter into the causal chain. There is a two-way connection between the facts and opinions prevailing at any moment in time: on the one hand participants seek to understand the situation (which includes both facts and opinions); on the other, they seek to influence the situation (which again includes both facts and opinions). The interplay between the cognitive and manipulative functions intrudes into the causal chain so that the chain does not lead directly from one set of facts to the next but reflects and affects the participants' views. Since those views do not correspond to the facts, they introduce an element of uncertainty into the course of events that is absent from natural phenomena. That element of uncertainty affects both the facts and the participants' views. Natural phenomena are not necessarily determined by scientific laws of universal validity, but social events are liable to be less so.

I explain the element of uncertainty inherent in social events by relying on the correspondence theory of truth and the concept of reflexivity. Reflexivity has been used in logic to refer to a relation that an object has to itself. I am using it in a somewhat different sense to describe a two-way connection between the participants' thinking and the situation in which they participate.

Knowledge is represented by true statements. A statement is true if and only if it corresponds to the facts. That is what the correspondence theory of truth tells us. To establish correspondence the facts and the statements which refer to them must be independent of each other. It is this requirement that cannot be fulfilled when we are part of the world we seek to understand. That is why participants cannot base their decisions on knowledge. What they lack in knowledge they have to make up for with guesswork based on experience, instinct, emotion, ritual, or other misconceptions. It is the participants' biased views and misconceptions that introduce an element of uncertainty into the course of events.

All this makes eminent sense. The puzzle is why the concept of reflexivity has not been generally recognized. In the case of the financial markets I know the answer: reflexivity prevents economists from producing theories that would explain and predict the behavior of financial markets in the same way that natural scientists can explain and predict natural phenomena. In order to establish and protect the status of economics as a science, economists have gone to great lengths to eliminate reflexivity from their subject matter. When it comes to other realms of reality, I am on less certain ground because I am less well grounded in philosophy. My impression is that philosophers have grappled with the problem in various ways. Aristotle, for instance, distinguished between theoretical reason (i.e., the cognitive function) and practical reason (i.e., the manipulative function). Being philosophers, however, they were so preoccupied with the cognitive function that they did not give sufficient weight to the manipulative function.

Philosophers recognized and explored the cognitive uncertainty associated with self-referent statements. The problem was first stated by the Cretan philosopher Epimenides when he said that Cretans always lie. The paradox of the liar eventually led Bertrand Russell to distinguish between statements that refer to themselves and those that do not. Analytical philosophers also studied the problems associated with speech acts, statements that make an impact on the situation to which they refer, but their interest was mainly focused on the cognitive aspect of the problem. The fact that social events have a different structure from natural phenomena did not receive widespread recognition. On the contrary, Karl Popper, who has been a major source of inspiration for me, declared the doctrine of the unity of method, that is to say, the same methods and criteria ought to apply to the study of natural events and social events. Of course, that is not the only point of view that has been put forward, but it is the prevailing view among social scientists who aspire to the same status as natural scientists. Not all social scientists do so. Anthropologists and most sociologists do not even try to imitate the natural sciences. But they are less influential than those who try.

The theory of reflexivity seeks to illuminate the relationship between thinking and reality. It applies to only a relatively narrow segment of reality. In the realm of natural phenomena, events occur independently of what anybody thinks; therefore, natural science can explain and predict the course of events with reasonable certainty. Reflexivity is confined to social phenomena—more specifically, those situations in which participants cannot base their decisions on knowledge—and it creates difficulties for the social sciences from which the natural sciences are exempt.

Reflexivity can be interpreted as a circularity, or two-way feedback loop, between the participants' views and the actual state of affairs. People base their decisions not on the actual situation that confronts them but on their perception or interpretation of that situation. Their decisions make an impact on the situation (the manipulative function), and changes in the situation are liable to change their perceptions (the cognitive function). The two functions operate concurrently, not sequentially. If the feedback were sequential, it would produce a uniquely determined sequence leading from facts to perceptions to new facts and then new perceptions, and so on. It is the fact that the two processes occur simultaneously that creates an indeterminacy in both the participants' perceptions and the actual course of events. This way of looking at reflexivity will be particularly useful, as we shall see, in understanding the behavior of financial markets. Whether we speak of a circularity, or a feedback mechanism, is a matter of interpretation; but the two-way interaction is real. The circularity is not an error of interpretation; on the contrary, it is the denial of a circularity that is the error. The theory of reflexivity seeks to correct that error.

The difficulties of the social sciences are only pale, second-hand reflections of the predicament in which the participants find themselves. They can affect the course of events—the future is influenced by their decisions—but they cannot base their decisions on knowledge. They are obliged to form a view of the world, but that view cannot possibly correspond to the actual state of affairs. Whether they recognize it or not, they are obliged to act on the basis of beliefs which are not rooted in reality. Misinterpretations of reality and other kinds of misconceptions play a much bigger role in determining the course of events than generally recognized. That is the main new insight that the theory of reflexivity has to offer. The current financial crisis will serve as a persuasive example.

Before expounding the theory in greater detail, I think it may help prepare the ground if I recount how I came to develop it over the years. As the reader will see, the theory grew out of my personal experience. I learned at an early age how ideologies based on false premises can transform reality. I also learned that there are times when the normal rules do not apply, and the abnormal becomes normal.

CHAPTER 2

Autobiography of
a Failed Philosopher

I have always been interested in philosophy. From an early age, I wanted to know who I was, the world into which I was born, the meaning of my life, and, even more, when I became aware of it, the prospect of my death. I started reading classical philosophers early in my teens, but the really important period came during the Nazi occupation of Hungary in 1944 and afterwards, when I emigrated to England in 1947.

The year 1944 was the formative experience of my life. I shall not give a detailed account of it because my father has done it better than I could.* Imagine a child of fourteen, coming from a middle-class background, suddenly confronted with the prospect of being deported and killed just because he is Jewish. Fortunately my father was well prepared for this far-from-equilibrium experience. He had lived through the Russian Revolution in Siberia, and that was the

---

*Tivadar Soros, *Masquerade: Dancing around Death in Nazi-Occupied Hungary* (New York: Arcade Publishing, 2001).

formative experience of *his* life. Until then he had been an ambitious young man. When World War I broke out, he volunteered to serve in the Austro-Hungarian army. He was captured by the Russians and taken as a prisoner of war to Siberia. Being ambitious, he became the editor of a newspaper produced by the prisoners. The paper was called *The Plank* because handwritten articles were posted on a plank; the authors hid behind the plank and listened to the comments made by the readers. My father became so popular that he was elected the prisoners' representative. When some soldiers escaped from a neighboring camp, their prisoners' representative was shot in retaliation. Instead of waiting for the same thing to happen in his camp, my father organized a group and led the breakout. His plan was to build a raft and sail down to the ocean, but his knowledge of geography was deficient; he did not know that all the rivers in Siberia flow into the Arctic Sea. They drifted for several weeks before they realized that they were heading to the Arctic, and it took them several months to make their way back to civilization across the taiga. In the meantime, the Russian Revolution broke out, and they became caught up in it. Only after a variety of adventures did my father manage to find his way back to Hungary; had he remained in the camp, he would have arrived home much sooner.

My father came home a changed man. His experiences during the Russian Revolution affected him profoundly. He lost his ambition and wanted nothing more from life than to enjoy it. He imparted to his children values that were very different from those of the milieu in which we lived. He had no desire to amass wealth or become socially prominent. On the contrary, he worked only as much as was necessary to make ends meet. I remember being sent to his main client to borrow some money before we went on a ski vacation; my father was grouchy for a few weeks afterwards because he had to pay it back. Although we were reasonably prosperous, we were not the typical bourgeois family, and we were proud of being different.

When the Germans occupied Hungary on March 19, 1944, my father knew these were not normal times and the normal rules did not apply. He arranged false identities for his family and a number of others. The clients paid; others received his help for free. Most of them survived. That was his finest hour.

Living with a false identity turned out to be an exhilarating experience for me. We were confronted by mortal danger, and people perished all around us, but we managed not only to survive but to emerge victorious because we were able to help so many others. We were on the side of the angels, and we triumphed against overwhelming odds. I was aware of the dangers, but I did not think they could touch me. It was high adventure, like living through *Raiders of the Lost Ark*. What more could a fourteen-year-old ask for?

After the heady adventures of the Nazi persecution, the situation began to deteriorate during the Soviet occupation. At first, the adventures continued, and we were able to maneuver successfully through perilous situations. The Swiss consulate employed my father to act as the liaison officer with the Russian occupying forces. The Swiss were looking after the Allied interests at the time, so this was a key position. When the Allied Powers established their own representative offices, my father retired because he felt that if he worked for the Allies he would be too exposed. It was a wise decision—he avoided later persecution. But the situation was becoming drab and oppressive for a youth who had become accustomed to adventure. I also thought that it was unhealthy for a young man of fifteen to think exactly like his fifty-year-old father. I told my father that I wanted to get away. "Where would you like to go?" he asked. "To Moscow, to find out about communism, or to London because of the BBC," I replied. "I know the Soviet Union intimately and I can tell you all about it," my father said. That left London. It was not easy to get there, but I arrived in September 1947.

Living in London was a comedown. I had no money and no friends. After my adventurous life, I was full of myself, but the people in London were not interested. I was an outsider looking in, and I discovered loneliness. There was a moment when I ran out of money. I was having a snack at a Lyons Corner House, and after paying for my food I had no money left. "I have touched bottom," I told myself, "and I am bound to rise. This will be a valuable experience."

I read and thought a lot while working as a swimming pool attendant in Brentford, waiting to be admitted to the London School of Economics (LSE). One of the books I read was Karl Popper's *The Open Society and Its Enemies*. That book struck me with the force of revelation. Popper argued that the Nazi and Communist ideologies have something in common—they both claim to be in possession of the ultimate truth. Since the ultimate truth is beyond human reach, both ideologies had to be based on a biased and distorted interpretation of reality; consequently, they could be imposed on society only by the use of repressive methods. He juxtaposed a different principle of social organization, one that is based on the recognition that the ultimate truth is beyond our reach and that we need institutions that allow people with different views and different interests to live together in peace. He called this principle the open society. Having just lived through the German and Soviet occupations, I became firmly committed to the ideal of an open society.

I also delved deeper into Popper's philosophy. Popper is first and foremost a philosopher of science. He maintained that scientific theories cannot be verified; they have to be treated as hypotheses subject to falsification; as long as they are not falsified, they can be accepted as provisionally true. The asymmetry between verification and falsification provides a solution to the otherwise intractable problem of induction: How can any number of discreet observations be used to verify a theory that claims to be universally valid? Replacing verification with falsification eliminates the need to use inductive logic. I consider this Popper's greatest contribution to the philosophy of science.

I was greatly influenced by Popper's philosophy, but of course I read many other books as well, and I did not accept all of Popper's positions uncritically. In particular, I disagreed with what he called the doctrine of the unity of method—that is to say that the same methods and criteria apply both in the natural and the social sciences. I maintain that there is a fundamental difference between the two, namely that the social sciences deal with events that have thinking participants. These participants base their decisions on their imperfect understanding. Their fallibility creates a difficulty for the understanding of social situations, which is absent in the case of natural phenomena. For that reason the social sciences need to use somewhat different methods and standards from the natural sciences. It may not be possible to draw a hard and fast dividing line between the two—for instance, where does evolutionary psychology or medicine belong? Nevertheless, as I explained in the previous chapter, the difference between natural and social phenomena plays a key role in my view of the world.

My philosophy evolved over the years, but I started forming it already as an undergraduate student at the LSE. I studied economic theory. I was not very good at math, and that led me to question the assumptions on which the mathematical models of economists were based. The theory of perfect competition assumed perfect knowledge, and that assumption was in direct conflict with Popper's contention that our understanding is inherently imperfect. In the course of its development, economic theory was forced to abandon the assumption of perfect knowledge, but it replaced that assumption with others that allowed economic theory to produce universally valid generalizations that were comparable to those of Isaac Newton in physics. The assumptions became increasingly convoluted and gave rise to an imaginary world that reflected only some aspects of reality but not others. That was the world of mathematical models describing a putative market equilibrium. I was more interested in the real world than in mathematical models, and that is what led me to develop the concept of reflexivity.

The theory of reflexivity does not yield determinate results comparable to Newtonian physics; rather, it identifies an element of indeterminacy which is inherent in situations that have participants who operate on the basis of imperfect understanding. Instead of a universal tendency towards equilibrium, financial markets follow a specific one-directional course. There may be patterns that tend to repeat themselves, but the actual course is indeterminate and unique. Thus, the theory of reflexivity constitutes a theory of history. However, the theory emphatically does not qualify as scientific because it does not provide deterministic explanations and predictions. It is merely a conceptual framework for understanding events that have human participants. Nevertheless, it served me well later when I became a market participant. Much later, when my success in the financial markets allowed me to set up a foundation, my theory of history guided me in my philanthropy.

My philosophical explorations did not help me much as a student. I barely passed my exams. I would have preferred to stay within the safe walls of academe—I even had a teaching assistant job prospect at the University of Michigan in Kalamazoo, but my grades were not good enough, and I was forced to go out into the real world. After several false starts, I ended up working as an arbitrage trader, first in London and then in New York.* At first I had to forget everything I had learned as a student in order to hold down my job, but eventually my college education came in very useful. In particular, I could apply my theory of reflexivity to establish a disequilibrium scenario or boom-bust pattern for financial markets. The rewarding part came when markets entered what I called far-from-equilibrium territory because that is when the generally accepted equilibrium models broke down. I specialized in detecting and playing far-from-equilibrium situations with good results. This led to my first pub-

---

*Arbitrage trading involves exploiting price discrepancies between interrelated markets. The discrepancies may occur between different locations, like Tokyo or Johannesburg versus New York, or different securities, like convertible bonds or warrants versus common stock.

lished book, *The Alchemy of Finance* (1987), in which I expounded my approach. I called it alchemy to emphasize that my theory does not meet the currently prevailing requirements of scientific method.

To what extent my financial success was due to my philosophy is a moot question because the salient feature of my theory is that it does not yield any firm predictions. Running a hedge fund involves the constant exercise of judgment in a risky environment, and that can be very stressful. I used to suffer from backaches and other psychosomatic ailments, and I received as many useful signals from my backaches as from my theory. Nevertheless, I attributed great importance to my philosophy and particularly my theory of reflexivity. Indeed, I considered it so significant, treasured it so much, that I found it difficult to part with it by putting it in writing and publishing it. No formulation was good enough.

To express my ideas in a few sentences, as I have done here, would have seemed sacrilegious. It had to be a book. As I belabored the points, my arguments became more and more convoluted until I reached a point when I could not understand what I had written the night before. As I have often recounted it, that is when I abandoned my philosophical explorations, returned to the land of the living, and started making money in earnest. But that, too, had its downside. When I resumed my philosophical investigations and published the results in *The Alchemy of Finance*, the philosophical part was dismissed by many critics as the self-indulgence of a successful speculator. That is how I came to consider myself a failed philosopher. Nevertheless, I kept on trying. Once I gave a lecture at the University of Vienna with the title "A Failed Philosopher Tries Again." I found myself in a large hall, looking down on the audience from a cathedra that towered high above the auditorium. I felt inspired by the setting to make an ex cathedra statement, and on the spur of the moment I announced the doctrine of fallibility. It was the best part of my lecture.

Some of the difficulties in formulating my ideas were inherent in the concepts of fallibility and reflexivity; others were self-inflicted. In retrospect, it is clear that I was not precise enough in my formulations and tended to overstate my case. As a result, the professionals whose positions I challenged could dismiss or ignore my arguments on technical grounds without giving them any real consideration. At the same time, some readers could look through my faulty rhetoric and appreciate the ideas that lay behind them. That was particularly true for people engaged in the financial markets, where my demonstrated success led them to look for the reason behind it, and the obscurity of my formulations added to their fascination. My publisher anticipated this and refrained from editing my manuscript. He wanted the book to be the subject of a cult. To this day *The Alchemy of Finance* is read by market participants, taught in business schools, but totally ignored in departments of economics.

Unfortunately, the idea that I was a failed philosopher came to be accepted by those who wrote about me, including my biographer, Michael Kaufman. He quoted my son Robert:

> My father will sit down and give you theories to explain why he does this or that. But I remember seeing it as a kid and thinking, Jesus Christ, at least half of this is bullshit. I mean, you know the reason he changes his position on the market or whatever is because his back starts

killing him. It has nothing to do with reason. He literally goes into a spasm, and it's this early warning sign.

If you're around him a long time, you realize that to a large extent he is driven by temperament. But he is always trying to rationalize what are basically his emotions. And he is living in a constant state of not exactly denial, but rationalization of his emotional state. And it's very funny.*

I harbored grave doubts myself. Although I took my philosophy very seriously, I was not at all certain that what I had to say deserved to be taken seriously by others. I knew that it was significant for me subjectively, but I was uncertain about its objective worth for others. The theory of reflexivity deals with a subject—the relationship between thinking and reality—that philosophers had been discussing for ages. Is it possible to say something new and original about it? After all, both the cognitive function and the participating function can be observed in real life; what can be so original in the concept of reflexivity? It must have been around under some other names. The fact that I am not well versed in the literature made it all the more difficult for me to reach a firm conclusion. Yet I desperately wanted to be taken seriously as a philosopher, and that very ambition turned into my greatest obstacle. I felt obliged to keep on explaining my philosophy because I felt it was not properly understood. All my books followed the same pattern. They recited my theory of history—usually at the end so as not to discourage the readers—

*Quoted in Michael Kaufman, *Soros: The Life and Times of a Messianic Billionaire* (New York: Alfred A. Knopf, 2002), 140.

and applied the theory to the present moment in history. With the passage of time, I overcame my reluctance to part with the concept of reflexivity, and the capsule versions of my philosophy became shorter and, I hope, clearer. In my last book, *The Age of Fallibility*, I put the philosophy up front. I resolved to make it the last presentation, for better or worse, but I was still not sure whether my philosophy deserved to be taken seriously.

Then something happened to change my mind. I was trying to answer the question, how could the propaganda techniques described in Orwell's *1984* be so successful in contemporary America? After all, in *1984* Big Brother was watching you; there was a Ministry of Truth and an apparatus of repression to take care of dissidents. In contemporary America there is freedom of thought and pluralistic media. Yet the Bush administration managed to mislead the people by using Orwellian Newspeak. Suddenly it dawned on me that the concept of reflexivity can shed new light on the question. Until then I had taken it for granted that Orwellian Newspeak could prevail only in a closed society like Orwell's *1984*. In doing so I was slavishly following Karl Popper's argument in favor of the open society, namely, that freedom of thought and expression is liable to lead to a better understanding of reality. His argument hinged on the unspoken assumption that political discourse aims at a better understanding of reality. But the concept of reflexivity asserts that there is such a thing as the manipulative (formerly participating) function, and political discourse can be successfully used to manipulate reality. Why, then, should politicians give preference to the cognitive over the manipulative function? That is appropriate for a social scientist whose aim is the acquisition of knowledge but not for a politician whose primary purpose is to get elected and stay in power.

This insight forced me to reconsider the concept of open society, which I had adopted from Karl Popper rather uncritically. But the insight also did something else. It convinced me that my conceptual framework has an objective value that goes beyond my personal predilection. The concepts of reflexivity and fallibility make an important contribution to our understanding, not because they are something novel or original by themselves but because they can be used to identify and refute widespread and influential misconceptions. One of those misconceptions is what I call the Enlightenment fallacy, which assumes that the purpose of reason is to produce knowledge. I call it a fallacy because it ignores the manipulative function. How deeply rooted the Enlightenment tradition is can be seen from my own experience. By embracing the concept of open society I subscribed to the Enlightenment fallacy even though by developing the concept of reflexivity I was asserting the importance of the manipulative function.

This conclusion removed the doubts I used to entertain about the objective value of my philosophy. Then came the financial crisis which is playing havoc with the financial system and threatens to engulf the economy. It is a vivid demonstration of how much damage misconceptions can cause. The theory of reflexivity offers a genuine alternative to the currently prevailing paradigm. If the theory of reflexivity is valid, the belief that financial markets tend towards equilibrium is false, and vice versa.

I am now ready to submit my conceptual framework to public consideration in the firm conviction that it deserves attention. I am aware of the various shortcomings in my previous presentations, which I hope to have overcome, and I believe that it will be worth the reader's while to make the effort required to understand my philosophy. Needless to say, this makes me very happy. I have been fortunate in making a lot of money and spending it well. But I have always wanted to be a philosopher, and finally I may have become one. What more can one ask for from one life?

CHAPTER 3

The Theory of Reflexivity

Some readers may find this chapter hard going. Those who are only interested in the financial markets may skip it or return to it after they have found my interpretation of the current situation convincing. From the author's perspective it remains indispensable—more important than the correct interpretation of the financial crisis.

FALLIBILITY

Having established the significance of my conceptual framework I can now dwell on some of the complexities I swept under the carpet in my summary presentation. I labored on my philosophy over many years. I shall now briefly recount the difficulties I encountered and summarize the conclusions I reached.

I did not make the relationship between fallibility and reflexivity sufficiently clear. People are participants, not just observers, and the knowledge they can acquire is not sufficient to guide them in their actions. They cannot base their decisions on knowledge alone. That is the condition I describe by the word "fallibility." Without fallibility there would be no reflexivity—if people could base their decisions on knowledge the element of uncertainty that characterizes reflexive situations would be removed—but fallibility is not confined to reflexive situations. In other words, fallibility is a more comprehensive condition, and reflexivity is a special case.

People's understanding is inherently imperfect because they are part of reality and a part cannot fully comprehend the whole. In calling our understanding imperfect, I mean that it is incomplete and, in ways that cannot be precisely defined, distorted. The human brain cannot grasp reality directly but only through the information it derives from it. The capacity of the human brain to process information is limited, whereas the amount of information that needs to be processed is practically infinite. The mind is obliged to reduce the available information to manageable proportions by using various techniques—generalizations, similes, metaphors, habits, rituals, and other routines. These techniques distort the underlying information but take on an existence of their own, further complicating reality and the task of understanding it.

Gaining knowledge requires a separation between thoughts and their object—facts must be independent of the statements that refer to them—and that separation is difficult to establish when you are part of what you seek to understand. One must put oneself in the position of a detached observer. The human mind has worked wonders in trying to reach that position, but in the end it cannot fully overcome the fact that it is part of the situation it seeks to comprehend.

Since I started developing my conceptual framework more than fifty years ago, cognitive science has made great progress in explaining how the human brain functions. I should like to invoke a couple of its main tenets because they provide an insight into our fallibility. One is that human consciousness is a relatively recent development and has been superimposed on the animal brain. The other is that reason and emotion are inseparable. These features are reflected in the language we use. Many of the most widely used metaphors have to do with the basic animal functions of vision and locomotion, and they carry an emotional connotation. Up and forward are good, down and backwards are bad; clear and bright are good, muddy and dark are bad. Ordinary language gives a very inexact and emotional view of the world, but it has an uncanny knack for identifying the features that are needed for instant decision making. Logic and mathematics are more precise and objective, but they are of limited use in coping with life. Ideas expressed in ordinary language do not constitute an exact representation of an underlying reality. They compound the complexity of the reality with which people have to cope in the course of their lives.

REFLEXIVITY

I analyzed the relationship between thinking and reality by introducing two functions that connect them in opposite directions. That is how I arrived at the concept of reflexivity.

But in trying to define and explain reflexivity I encountered enormous difficulties. I drew a distinction between thinking and reality, whereas what I wanted to say was that thinking is part of reality. I found myself talking about a two-way connection between the course of events and the participants' thinking. That left out a two-way connection between the thinking of the various participants. To take that connection into account I found myself obliged to distinguish between the objective and subjective aspects of reality. The former refers to the course of events, the latter to the participants' thinking. There is only one objective aspect, but there are as many subjective aspects as there are participants. The direct interpersonal relations among participants are more likely to be reflexive than the interaction between perceptions and events because events take longer to unfold.

Once we distinguish between objective and subjective aspects we must also distinguish between reflexive processes and reflexive statements. Reflexive statements belong to the realm of direct interpersonal relations, and those relations are more likely to be reflexive than the course of events.

Consider a statement about the objective aspect: "It is raining." That is either true or false; it is not reflexive. But take a statement like: "You are my enemy." That may be true or false, depending on how you react to it. That is reflexive. Reflexive statements resemble self-referent statements, but the indeterminacy is inherent not in their meaning but in the impact they make. The most famous self-referent statement is the paradox of the liar: "Cretans always lie," said Epimenides. If this statement is true, the Cretan philosopher was not lying, and therefore the statement is false. The ambivalence has nothing to do with the impact of the statement. By contrast, in "You are my enemy" the truth value of the statement depends on your reaction.

In the case of reflexive processes the indeterminacy is introduced by a lack of correspondence between the objective and subjective aspects of a situation. A situation may be reflexive even if the cognitive and manipulative functions operate sequentially and not simultaneously. The process then evolves over a period of time, but it qualifies as reflexive as long as neither the participants' thinking nor the actual state of affairs remains the same at the end of the process as it was at the beginning, and the changes occur as a result of some misconception or misinterpretation by the participants, introducing an element of genuine indeterminacy into the course of events. This renders the situation unpredictable on the basis of scientific laws.

Reflexivity is best demonstrated and studied in the financial markets because financial markets are supposed to be governed by such laws. In other areas the science is less well developed. Even in the financial markets demonstrably reflexive processes occur only intermittently. On a day-by-day basis markets seem to follow certain statistical rules, but occasionally those rules are broken. We may therefore distinguish between humdrum, everyday events that are predictable, and reflexive processes that are not. The latter are of great significance because they alter the course of history. This consideration led me to argue that historic developments are distinguished from everyday events by their reflexivity. But that argument is false. There are many historic events, such as earthquakes, that are not reflexive. The distinction between humdrum and reflexive turns out to be tautological: reflexive developments leave neither the objective nor the subjective aspects of reality unaltered, by definition.

Now that cognitive science and the study of languages have made such progress the concept of reflexivity has been to some extent superseded. Reflexivity distinguishes only two functions: the cognitive and the manipulative. This is a rather crude classification compared to the much more nuanced and detailed analyses of brain and language functions that have become available in recent years. Nevertheless, the concept has not lost its relevance. It pinpoints a distortion in the way philosophers and scientists tend to look at the world. Their primary concern is the cognitive function; insofar as the manipulative function interferes with the proper functioning of cognition, they are inclined to ignore it or to deliberately eliminate it from consideration. Economic theory provides the best example. The theory of perfect competition was built on the assumption of perfect knowledge. When the assumption proved untenable, economists went through ever more elaborate contortions in order to protect the edifice they have erected against the nefarious effects of reflexivity. That is how the assumption of perfect knowledge morphed into the theory of rational expectations—a make-believe world that bears no resemblance to reality. More on that in the next chapter.

The Human Uncertainty Principle

The distinguishing feature of reflexivity is that it introduces an element of uncertainty into the participants' thinking and an element of indeterminacy into the situation in which they participate. Reflexivity bears some resemblance to Werner Heisenberg's uncertainty principle in quantum physics, but there is one important difference: quantum physics deals with phenomena that do not have thinking participants. Heisenberg's discovery of the uncertainty principle did not change the behavior of quantum particles or waves one iota, but the recognition of reflexivity may alter human behavior. Thus, the uncertainty associated with reflexivity affects not only the participants but also the social scientists who seek to establish universally valid laws governing human behavior. This additional element of uncertainty may be described as the human uncertainty principle, and it complicates the task of the social sciences.

THE ENLIGHTENMENT FALLACY

Most of the difficulties I encountered in discussing reflexivity are due to the fact that I had to use a language that does not recognize its existence. I tried to show a two-way interconnection between the participants' thinking and the situation in which they participate, but Western intellectual tradition went out of its way to separate thinking and reality. The effort resulted in dichotomies like those between mind and body, Platonic ideals and observable phenomena, ideas and material conditions, statements and facts. The distinction I have introduced between the subjective and objective aspects of reality falls into the same category.

It is understandable how these dichotomies come into existence: The objective of the cognitive function is to produce knowledge. Knowledge requires statements that correspond to the facts. To establish correspondence, statements and facts have to be treated as separate categories. Hence the pursuit of knowledge leads to the separation of thinking and reality. This dualism had it roots in Greek philosophy, and it came to dominate our view of the world during the Enlightenment.

The philosophers of the Enlightenment put their faith in reason; they saw reality as something separate and independent of reason, and they expected reason to provide a full and accurate picture of reality. Reason was supposed to work like a searchlight, illuminating a reality that lay there, passively awaiting discovery. The possibility that the decisions of thinking agents could influence the situation was left out of account because that would have interfered with the separation between thoughts and their object. In other words, the Enlightenment failed to recognize reflexivity. It postulated an imaginary world where the manipulative function could not interfere with the cognitive function. Indeed, it failed to recognize the manipulative function altogether. It assumed that the sole purpose of thinking was to pursue knowledge. "Cogito ergo sum," said René Descartes. Descartes departed from Aristotle by focusing exclusively on theoretical reason, neglecting what Aristotle called practical reason and I call the manipulative function. This resulted in a distorted view of reality but one that was appropriate to the age when it was formulated.

At the time of the Enlightenment, humankind had relatively little knowledge of or control over the forces of nature, but scientific method held out infinite promise because it was beginning to produce significant results. It was appropriate to think of reality as something out there waiting to be discovered. After all, not even the earth had been fully explored in the eighteenth century. Gathering facts and establishing the relationships among them was richly rewarding. Knowledge was being acquired in so many different ways and from so many different directions that the possibilities seemed unlimited. Reason was sweeping away centuries of superstition and generating in its place a triumphant sense of progress.

The Enlightenment, as it came to be understood, recognized no limit to the acquisition of knowledge. Having identified only a one-way connection between thinking and reality, it treated reality as something independently given that could be fully understood by making statements that corresponded to the facts. This point of view—Popper called it comprehensive rationality—reached its apogee in logical positivism, a philosophy that flourished at the beginning of the twentieth century, primarily in Vienna. Logical positivism held that only empirical statements that could be verified were meaningful, and metaphysical discussions were meaningless.* Logical positivists treated facts and statements as if they belonged to separate universes. The only connection between the two universes was that true statements corresponded to the facts and false statements did not. In these circumstances the facts served as a reliable criterion of truth. This was the foundation of the correspondence theory of truth. The possibility that statements also constituted facts was largely, but not entirely, ignored. A lot of attention was paid to the paradox of the liar.

Bertrand Russell, the British philosopher who was responsible for bringing Ludwig Wittgenstein to Cambridge from Vienna, offered a solution to the paradox of the liar.

*Logical positivists made an exception for analytic statements such as "bachelors are unmarried males," which they considered meaningful. This cleared the way to analytical philosophy.

Russell drew a distinction between two classes of statements: self-referential statements and non-self-referential ones. Since the truth value of self-referent statements could not be unequivocally determined, he proposed that they should be excluded from the universe of meaningful statements. This solution might have served to preserve the pristine separation between facts and statements, but it would have prevented people from thinking about issues that concerned them, or even from being conscious of themselves. The absurdity of this position was highlighted by Wittgenstein, who concluded his *Tractatus Logico-Philosophicus* by stating that those who understood the book had to realize that it was meaningless. Shortly thereafter, Wittgenstein abandoned the pursuit of an ideal logical language and replaced it with a study of the workings of ordinary language.

Fertile Fallacies

While the Enlightenment's faith in reason was not fully justified, it produced truly impressive results, which were sufficient to sustain the Enlightenment for two centuries. I call flawed ideas that produce positive results fertile fallacies. I call the separation of thinking and reality a fertile fallacy. It is not the only one. Fertile fallacies abound in history. I contend that all cultures are built on fertile fallacies. They are fertile because they flourish and produce positive results before their deficiencies are discovered; they are fallacies because our understanding of reality is inherently imperfect. We are, of course, capable of acquiring knowledge; but if that knowledge proves useful we are liable to overexploit it and extend it to areas where it no longer applies. That is when it becomes a fallacy. That is what happened to the Enlightenment. The ideas of the Enlightenment have become deeply ingrained in our Western civilization, and are difficult to shake. They permeate the writings even of those who are critical of some aspects of the Enlightenment tradition, including myself.

POPPER'S SCHEME
OF SCIENTIFIC METHOD

Karl Popper, a non-card-carrying member of the Vienna Circle, was critical of Wittgenstein and disagreed with comprehensive rationality. He maintained that reason is not capable of establishing the truth of generalizations beyond doubt. Even scientific laws cannot be verified because it is impossible to derive universally valid generalizations from individual observations, however numerous, by deductive logic. Scientific method works best by adopting an attitude of comprehensive skepticism: Scientific laws should be treated as hypotheses which are provisionally valid unless and until they are falsified.

Popper constructed a beautifully simple and elegant scheme of scientific method consisting of three elements and three operations. The three elements are the initial conditions, the final conditions, and the generalizations of universal validity, or scientific laws. The three operations are prediction, explanation, and testing. When the initial conditions are combined with scientific laws they provide a prediction. When the final conditions are combined with those laws they provide an explanation. In this sense, predictions and explanations are symmetrical and reversible.

What is missing from this scheme is the verification of the laws. Here comes Popper's special contribution to our understanding of scientific method. He asserted that scientific laws cannot be verified; they can only be falsified. That is the role of testing. Scientific laws can be tested by pairing off initial conditions with final conditions. If they fail to conform to the scientific law in question, that law has been falsified. Statements that are not subject to falsification do not qualify as scientific. One nonconforming instance may be sufficient to destroy the validity of the generalization, but no amount of conforming instances are sufficient to verify a generalization beyond any doubt. In this sense, there is an asymmetry between verification and falsification. The symmetry between prediction and explanation, the asymmetry between verification and falsification, and the role of testing are the three salient features of Popper's scheme.

Popper's contention that scientific laws cannot be verified resolves the otherwise insoluble problem of induction. Just because the sun has risen in the east every day since man can remember, how can we be sure that it will continue to do so? Popper's scheme removes the need for verification by treating scientific laws as provisionally valid until and unless they have been falsified. Generalizations that cannot be falsified do not qualify as scientific. This interpretation emphasizes the central role that testing plays in scientific method. It establishes a case for critical thinking that allows science to grow, improve, and innovate.

Many features of Popper's scheme have been criticized by professional philosophers. For instance, Popper maintains that the more severe the testing, the greater the value of the generalization that survives it. Professional philosophers question whether the severity of tests and the value of generalizations can be measured. Nevertheless, Popper's assertion makes perfect sense to me, and I can prove it by invoking my experience in the stock market. In the savings and loan crisis of 1986 there were grave doubts whether a mortgage insurance company, Mortgage Guaranty Insurance (nicknamed MAGIC), would be able to survive. The stock fell precipitously, and I bought it in the belief that its business model was sound enough to withstand a severe test. I was right, and I made a killing. Generally speaking, the more an investment thesis is at odds with the generally prevailing view, the greater the financial rewards one can reap if it turns out to be correct. It is on these grounds that I can claim that I accept Popper's scheme more wholeheartedly than the professional philosophers.

ABANDONING THE UNITY OF METHOD

Yet, in spite of his insight that the ultimate truth is beyond the reach of reason, Popper insisted on what he called the doctrine of the unity of scientific method, namely, the same methods and criteria apply to the study of social affairs as to the study of natural phenomena. How could that be? The participants in social affairs act on the basis of fallible understanding. Their fallibility introduces an element of uncertainty into social affairs that does not afflict the study of natural phenomena. The difference needs to be recognized.

I sought to express the difference by introducing the concept of reflexivity. The concept of self-reference had already been extensively analyzed by Russell and others. But self-reference pertains exclusively to the realm of statements. If the separation between the universe of statements and the universe of facts is a distortion of reality, then there has to be a similar effect in the realm of facts. That is the relationship that the concept of reflexivity seeks to express. To some extent the concept was explored by J. L. Austin and John Searle in their work on speech acts, but I see it in a much wider context. Reflexivity is a two-way feedback mechanism that affects not only statements (by rendering their truth value indeterminate) but also facts (by introducing an element of indeterminacy into the course of events).

Yet, in spite of my preoccupation with the concept of reflexivity, I failed to recognize a flaw in Popper's concept of open society: that political discourse is not necessarily directed at the pursuit of truth. I believe both Popper and I made these mistakes because of *our* preoccupation with the pursuit of truth. Fortunately, these errors are not fatal because the case for critical thinking remains unimpaired and the mistakes can be corrected: we can recognize a difference between the natural and social sciences, and we can introduce the pursuit of truth as a requirement for an open society.

The postmodern attitude towards reality is much more dangerous. While it has stolen a march on the Enlightenment by discovering that reality can be manipulated, it does not recognize the pursuit of truth as a requirement. Consequently, it allows the manipulation of reality to go unhindered. Why is that so dangerous? Because in the absence of proper understanding the results of the manipulation are liable to be radically different from the expectations of the manipulators. One of the most successful instances of manipulation was when President George W. Bush declared a War on Terror and used it to invade Iraq on false pretenses. The outcome was the exact opposite of what he intended: He wanted to demonstrate American supremacy and garner political support in the process; but he caused a precipitous decline in American power and influence and lost political support in the process.

To guard against the dangers of manipulation, the concept of open society originally formulated by Karl Popper needs to be modified in an important respect. What Popper took for granted needs to be introduced as an explicit requirement. Popper assumed that the purpose of critical thinking is to gain a better understanding of reality. That is true in science but not in politics. The primary purpose of political discourse is to gain power and to stay in power. Those who fail to recognize this are unlikely to *be* in power. The only way in which politicians can be persuaded to pay more respect to reality is by the electorate insisting on it, rewarding those whom it considers truthful and insightful, and punishing those who engage in deliberate deception. In other words, the electorate needs to be more committed to the pursuit of truth than it is at present. Without such a commitment, democratic politics will not produce the desired results. An open society can be only as virtuous as the people living in it.

The Pursuit of Truth

Now that we know reality can be manipulated, it is much more difficult to make a commitment to the pursuit of truth than it was at the time of the Enlightenment. For one thing, it is more difficult to establish what the truth is. The Enlightenment regarded reality as something independently given and therefore knowable; but when the course of events is contingent on the biased beliefs and misconceptions of the participants, reality turns into a moving target. For another, it is not at all self-evident why the pursuit of truth should take precedence over the pursuit of power. And even if the electorate were convinced of it, how can the politicians be kept honest?

Reflexivity provides part of the answer, even if it leaves the problem of keeping politicians honest unresolved. It teaches us that the pursuit of truth is important exactly because misconceptions are liable to lead to unintended adverse consequences. Unfortunately the concept of reflexivity is not properly understood. That can be seen from the far-reaching influence that the Enlightenment tradition and, more recently, the postmodern idiom have exerted over people's view of the world. Both interpretations of the relationship between thinking and reality are distorted. The Enlightenment ignores the manipulative function. The postmodern approach goes to the other extreme: By treating reality as a collection of often conflicting narratives, it fails to give sufficient weight to the objective aspect of reality. The concept of reflexivity helps to identify what is missing from each. That said, reflexivity is far from a perfect representation of a very complex reality. The main problem with the concept is that it seeks to describe the relationship between thinking and reality as separate entities when in reality thinking is part of reality.

I have gained a healthy respect for the objective aspect of reality both by having lived under Nazi and Communist regimes and by speculating in the financial markets. The only experience that teaches you more respect for an external reality that is beyond your control than losing money in the financial markets is death—and death is not an actual experience during one's lifetime. It is much harder for a public that spends much of its time in the virtual reality of television shows, video games, and other forms of entertainment to develop such respect. It is noteworthy that people in America go to great lengths to deny or forget about death. Yet if you disregard reality it is liable to catch up with you. What better time to bring this argument home than the present, when the unintended adverse consequences of the War on Terror are so clearly visible, and the virtual reality of synthetic financial products has disrupted our financial system?

The Postmodern Idiom

I had not paid much attention to the postmodern point of view until recently. I did not study it, and I did not fully understand it, but I was willing to dismiss it out of hand because it seemed to conflict with the concept of reflexivity. I treated the postmodern view of the world as an overreaction to the Enlightenment's excessive faith in reason, namely, the belief that reason is capable of fully comprehending reality. I did not see any direct connection between the postmodern idiom and totalitarian ideologies and closed societies, although I could see that, by being extremely permissive of different points of view, the postmodern position might encourage the rise of totalitarian ideologies. Recently, I changed my views. I now see a direct connection between the postmodern idiom and the Bush administration's ideology. That insight came from an October 2004 article by Ron Suskind in the *New York Times Magazine*. This is what he wrote:

> In the summer of 2002 . . . I had a meeting with a senior adviser to Bush. He expressed the White House's displeasure [about a biography of Paul O'Neill, *The Price of Loyalty* by Ron Suskind*], and then he told me something that at the time I didn't fully comprehend—but which I now believe gets to the very heart of the Bush presidency.
>
> The aide said that guys like me were "in what we call the reality-based community," which he defined as people who "believe that solutions emerge from your judicious study of discernible reality." I nodded and murmured something about enlightenment principles and empiricism. He cut me off. "That's not the way the world really works anymore," he continued. "We're an empire now, and when we act, we create our own reality. And while you're studying that reality—judiciously, as you will—we'll act again, creating other new realities, which you can study too, and that's how things will sort out. We're history's actors . . . and you, all of you, will be left to just study what we do."†

The aide, presumably Karl Rove, did not merely recognize that the truth can be manipulated, he promoted the ma-

---

*Ron Suskind, *The Price of Loyalty: George W. Bush, the White House, and the Education of Paul O'Neill* (New York: Simon & Schuster, 2004).

†Ron Suskind, "Without a Doubt," *New York Times Magazine*, October 17, 2004, 51.

nipulation of truth as a superior approach. This interferes directly with the pursuit of truth both by declaring it futile and by making the task more difficult through constant manipulation. Moreover, Rove's approach led to the restriction of liberties by using the manipulation of public opinion to enhance the powers and prerogatives of the president. That is what the Bush administration wrought by declaring the War on Terror.

I believe the War on Terror provides an excellent illustration of the dangers inherent in Rove's ideology. The Bush administration used the War on Terror to invade Iraq. This was one of the most successful instances of manipulation, yet its consequences for the United States and the Bush administration itself were nothing short of disastrous.

The public is now awakening, as if from a bad dream. What can it learn from the experience? That reality is a hard task master, and we manipulate it at our peril: The consequences of our actions are liable to diverge from our expectations. However powerful we are, we cannot impose our will on the world: we need to understand the way the world works. Perfect knowledge is not within our reach; but we must try to come as close to it as we can. Reality is a moving target, yet we need to pursue it. In short, understanding reality ought to take precedence over manipulating it.

As things stand now, the pursuit of power tends to take precedence over the pursuit of truth. Popper and his followers—including me—made a mistake when we took the pursuit of truth for granted. Recognizing the mistake should not lead us to abandon the concept of open society. On the contrary, the experience with the Bush administration ought to reinforce our commitment to open society as a desirable form of social organization. We must alter, however, our definition of what an open society entails. In addition to the familiar attributes of a liberal democracy—free elections, individual liberties, division of powers, the rule of law, etc.—it also entails an electorate that insists on certain standards of honesty and truthfulness. What these standards are need to be first carefully elaborated and then generally accepted.

Standards of Political Discourse

Karl Popper, who was first and foremost a philosopher of science, elaborated such standards for scientific discourse and experimentation. To give just one example, laws need to be falsifiable, and experiments need to be replicable to qualify as scientific. The standards of scientific method cannot be applied to politics directly; nevertheless, they serve as an example of the kind of rules that need to be established.

We have identified two crucial differences between science and politics. One is that politics is more concerned with the pursuit of power than the pursuit of truth. The other is that in science there is an independent criterion, namely the facts, by which the truth or validity of statements can be judged. In politics, the facts are often contingent on the participants' decisions. Reflexivity throws a monkey wrench into Popper's model of scientific method.

In *The Alchemy of Finance*, I took issue with Popper's doctrine of the unity of method. I argued that reflexivity prevents the social sciences from meeting the standards of natural science. How could scientific method be expected to produce generalizations which reversibly provide determi-

nate predictions and explanations, when the course of
is inherently indeterminate? We must be content with
hunches and alternative scenarios instead of determinate
predictions. In retrospect, I probably spent too much time
on examining the role of the social scientists and not enough
on the participants in social situations. That is why I failed to
recognize a flaw in Popper's concept of open society, namely,
that politics is more concerned with the pursuit of power
than the pursuit of truth. I am now correcting the error by
introducing truthfulness and respect for reality as explicit requirements for an open society.

Unfortunately I do not have any clear-cut formula for how
that requirement could be met; I can only identify it as an un-
solved problem. That is not surprising. The problem is not
one that an individual can solve; it requires a change in the
attitude of the public.*

I believe political discourse used to abide by much higher
standards of truthfulness and respect for the opponents'
opinions in the first two hundred years of democracy in
America than it does today. I realize that old men usually see
the past in rosier colors than the present, but in this case I believe I can justify my claim by invoking the Enlightenment
fallacy. As long as people believed in the power of reason
they also believed in the pursuit of truth. Now that we have
discovered that reality can be manipulated, that belief has
been shaken.

This leads to the paradoxical conclusion that the higher
standards in politics were based on an illusion, and they were

*Bernard Williams has a valuable discussion of the point in his book *Truth and
Truthfulness: An Essay in Genealogy* (Princeton: Princeton University Press,
2004).

undermined by the discovery of a truth, namely, that reality can be manipulated. This conclusion is reinforced by the fact that Rove was able to write circles around those who still labored under the Enlightenment fallacy and sought to prevail by rational arguments rather than by appealing to the emotions without any regard for the facts. The War on Terror proved to be the most effective slogan of all because it appealed to the strongest of emotions, the fear of death.

To reestablish those higher standards that used to prevail, people must come to realize that reality matters even if it can be manipulated. In other words, people must come to terms with reflexivity. This is no easy task, because a reflexive reality is much more complicated than the reality that the Enlightenment was pursuing. Indeed reality is so complicated that it can never be fully known. Nevertheless, it remains just as important to gain better understanding as it was at the time of the Enlightenment, and in this respect coming to terms with reflexivity would constitute an important step forward. That was the point I was trying to make in my last book when I said that we need to advance from the Age of Reason to the Age of Fallibility.

Radical Fallibility

Fallibility and reflexivity are difficult ideas to accept and to work with. As participants we are constantly called upon to make decisions and to act. But how can we act with any degree of confidence when we may be wrong and our actions may have unintended adverse consequences? It would be much more desirable if we could rely on a doctrine or belief system that lays claim to the ultimate truth. Unfortunately what is desirable is not attainable; the ultimate truth is beyond the reach of the human intellect. Ideologies that promise absolute certainty are bound to be wrong. Only this insight can stop people from adopting such an ideology.

The fact that the ultimate truth is unattainable does not rule out religion. On the contrary, where the ability to obtain knowledge stops, the scope for beliefs opens up. To assert that we cannot base our decisions on knowledge is tantamount to admitting that we cannot avoid relying on beliefs, religious or secular. Indeed, religion has played an important role throughout history. The period since the Enlightenment constitutes an exception. The faith in reason temporarily eclipsed religion. That is how the twentieth century came to be dominated by secular ideologies: socialism, communism, fascism, national socialism, and I am tempted to add capitalism and the belief in markets. Now that the fallacious element in the Enlightenment view of the world has become more obvious, religious beliefs have once again come to the fore.

Science cannot disprove religious or secular ideologies because it is in the nature of such ideologies that they are not subject to falsification. Nevertheless, we are well advised to act on the assumption that we may be wrong. Even if a dogma cannot be proven wrong, our interpretation cannot be proven right.

So far I am following in Popper's footsteps. I am inclined to go a step further. He asserts that we *may* be wrong. I adopt as my working hypothesis that we are *bound* to be wrong. I call this the postulate of radical fallibility. I base it on the following argument: We are capable of acquiring some insight into reality, but the more we understand, the more there is to be understood. Confronted by this moving target, we are liable to overburden whatever knowledge we have acquired by extending it to areas where it is no longer applicable. In this way, even valid interpretations of reality are bound to give rise to distorted ones. This argument is similar to the Peter Principle, which holds that competent employees are promoted until they reach their level of incompetence.

I find my position buttressed by the findings of cognitive linguistics. George Lakoff, among others, has shown that language employs metaphors rather than strict logic. Metaphors work by transferring observations or attributes from one set of circumstances to another, and it is almost inevitable that the process will be carried too far. This can be best seen in the case of scientific method. Science is a highly successful method for acquiring knowledge. As such, it seems to contradict the postulate of radical fallibility, namely, that we are bound to be wrong. But the process has been carried too far. Because of the success of natural science, social scientists have gone to great lengths to imitate natural science.

Consider classical economic theory. In its use of the concept of equilibrium, it is imitating Newtonian physics. But in financial markets, where expectations play an important role, the contention that markets tend towards equilibrium does not correspond to reality. Rational expectations theory has gone through great contortions to create an artificial world in which equilibrium prevails, but in that world reality is fitted to the theory rather than the other way round. This is a case to which the postulate of radical fallibility applies.

Even when they failed to meet the rules and standards of scientific method, social thinkers sought to cloak their theories in scientific guise to gain acceptance. Sigmund Freud and Karl Marx both asserted that their theories determined the course of events in their respective fields *because* they were scientific. (At that time, scientific laws were expected to be deterministic.) Popper was successful in unmasking them, particularly Marx, by showing that their theories could not be tested in accordance with his scheme; therefore they were not scientific. But Popper did not go far enough. He did not acknowledge that the study of social phenomena encounters an obstacle that is absent in the natural sciences—reflexivity and the human uncertainty principle. As a consequence, the slavish imitation of natural science does not produce an adequate representation of reality. General equilibrium and rational expectations are far removed from reality. They provide examples of how an approach that produces valid results becomes overexploited and overburdened to the point where it is no longer valid.

Suppose my objections to the concepts of general equilibrium and rational expectations were generally upheld, and the theories were abandoned; they would no longer serve as examples of radical fallibility. This shows the fatal flaw in my postulate: It is not necessarily true. Just as Popper did not go far enough, I went too far. We are not bound to be wrong in every situation. Misconceptions can be corrected.

Where does that leave my postulate? It qualifies as a fertile fallacy. It cannot possibly be true because if it were true it would fall into the category of the paradox of the liar. If it were a scientific theory it would be proven false because in Popper's scheme a single instance is sufficient to falsify a theory. But the postulate of radical fallibility is not a scientific theory. It is a working hypothesis and, as such, it works remarkably well. It helps to identify initially self-reinforcing but eventually self-defeating sequences because it presupposes that ideas that work well will be overexploited to the point where they do not work anymore. Indeed, in the course of my investment career I identified many more boom-bust sequences than actually occurred. I discarded most of them by a process of trial and error. The postulate of radical fallibility emphasizes the divergence between reality and the participants' perception of reality, and it focuses attention on misconceptions as a causal factor in history. This leads to a particular interpretation of history that can be illuminating. The present moment is such a time. I regard the War on Terror as a misconception, or false metaphor, that has had a nefarious effect on America and the world. And the current financial crisis can be directly attributed to a false interpretation of how financial markets function.

The postulate of radical fallibility and the idea of fertile fallacies are the hallmarks of my thinking. These concepts sound negative, but they are not. What is imperfect can be improved; radical fallibility leaves infinite room for improvement. In my definition, an open society is an imperfect society that holds itself open to improvement. Open society engenders hope and creativity, although open society is constantly endangered, and history is full of disappointments. In spite of the negative-sounding terminology—imperfect understanding, radical fallibility, fertile fallacies—my outlook on life is profoundly optimistic. That is because from time to time my conceptual framework allowed me to bring about improvements in real life.

CHAPTER 4

Reflexivity in Financial Markets

So far I have delved into the realm of abstractions. I asserted that there is a two-way connection between thinking and reality which, when it operates simultaneously, introduces an element of uncertainty into the participants' thinking and an element of indeterminacy into the course of events. I called this two-way connection reflexivity, and I asserted that reflexivity distinguishes unique, historical developments from humdrum, everyday events. Now I must provide some concrete evidence that such reflexive developments actually occur and that they are historically significant.

For this purpose, I shall turn first not to political history but to the financial markets. The financial markets offer an excellent laboratory because most of the price and other data are public and quantified. There are plenty of reflexive processes in political and other forms of history as well, but they are more difficult to demonstrate and analyze. The main advantage of financial markets as a laboratory is that my theory of reflexivity is in direct contradiction of a theory that is still widely accepted, namely, the belief that financial markets tend towards equilibrium. If equilibrium theory is correct, reflexivity cannot exist. By the same token, if the theory of reflexivity is correct, equilibrium theory is invalid. The behavior of financial markets needs to be interpreted as a somewhat unpredictable historical process rather than one determined by timelessly valid laws. If that interpretation is accepted for financial markets it can then be extended to other forms of history where reflexivity is less easily observed.

I first published my theory about financial markets in *The Alchemy of Finance*, but the theory of reflexivity did not receive any serious critical consideration. The situation is changing. Economists realize that the prevailing paradigm is inadequate, but they have not yet developed a new one. The subprime mortgage bubble that burst in August 2007 and caused widespread financial dislocations is liable to force the pace. I believe reflexivity as a phenomenon is about to gain much wider recognition, and my theory offers an important insight. The reflexive processes currently unfolding in the financial markets and the global economy constitute an important element in the reality that confronts us at the present moment in history. The danger that they will not be properly understood is very great. That is yet another instance where the cognitive function needs to be given precedence over the manipulative one in order to avoid adverse consequences. I shall summarize my theory in general terms here and apply it to the current situation in Part 2.

Equilibrium Theory

Economic theory seeks to imitate the natural sciences. It aims at establishing timelessly valid generalizations that can be used reversibly to explain and predict economic phenomena. In particular the theory of perfect competition modeled itself after Newtonian physics by specifying the equilibrium between supply and demand towards which market prices tend. The theory has been constructed as an axiomatic system like Euclidean geometry: It is based on postulates, and all of its conclusions are derived from them by logical or mathematical calculation. The postulates specify certain ideal conditions, yet the conclusions are supposed to be relevant to the real world. The theory holds that under the specified conditions the unrestrained pursuit of self-interest leads to the optimum allocation of resources. The equilibrium point is reached when each firm produces at a level where its marginal cost equals the market price, and each consumer buys an amount whose marginal utility equals the market price. It can be mathematically calculated that the equilibrium position maximizes the benefit of all participants. It is this line of argument that served as the theoretical underpinning for the *laissez-faire* policies of the nineteenth century, and it is also the basis of the belief in the "magic of the marketplace" that gained widespread acceptance during Ronald Reagan's presidency.

One of the key postulates of the theory as it was originally proposed is perfect knowledge. Other postulates include homogeneous and divisible products and a large enough number of participants so that no individual buyer or seller can influence the market price. The assumption of perfect knowledge was in direct conflict not only with reflexivity but also with the idea of imperfect understanding, convincingly argued by Karl Popper. That is what made me question the theory as a student. Classical economists used the concept of perfect knowledge in exactly that sense in which Popper objected to it. They were laboring under what I now call the Enlightenment fallacy. As the epistemological problems began to surface, exponents of the theory found that they had to use a more modest concept: information. In its modern formulation the theory merely postulates perfect information.*

Unfortunately this assumption is not quite sufficient to support the conclusions of the theory. To make up for the deficiency, modern economists resorted to an ingenious device: they insisted that the demand and supply curves should be taken as independently given. They did not present this as a postulate; rather, they based their claim on methodological grounds. They argued that the task of economics is to study the relationship between supply and demand and not either by itself. Demand may be a suitable subject for psychologists, supply may be the province of engineers or management scientists; both are beyond the scope of economics.† Therefore, both must be taken as given. This was the theory I was taught as a student.

Yet, if we stop to ask what it means that the conditions of supply and demand are independently given, it becomes clear that an additional assumption has been introduced. Otherwise, where would those curves come from? We are dealing with an assumption disguised as a methodological device. Participants are supposed to choose between alternatives in accordance with their scale of preferences. The un-

---

*George Stigler, *Theory of Price* (New York: Macmillan, 1966).

†Lionel C. Robbins, *An Essay on the Nature and Significance of Economic Science*, 3d ed. (New York: New York University Press, 1984).

spoken assumption is that the participants *know* what those preferences and alternatives are.

As I shall try to show, this assumption is untenable. The shape of the supply and demand curves cannot be taken as independently given because both of them incorporate the participants' expectations about events that are shaped by their own expectations. Nowhere is the role of expectations more clearly visible than in financial markets. Buy and sell decisions are based on expectations about future prices, and future prices, in turn, are contingent on present buy and sell decisions.

To speak of supply and demand as if they were determined by forces that are independent of the market participants' expectations is quite misleading. Demand and supply curves are presented in textbooks as though they were grounded in empirical evidence. But there is scant evidence for independently given demand and supply curves. Anyone who trades in markets where prices are continuously changing knows that participants are very much influenced by market developments. Rising prices often attract buyers and vice versa. How could self-reinforcing trends persist if supply and demand curves were independent of market prices? Yet, even a cursory look at commodity, stock, and currency markets confirms that such trends are the rule rather than the exception.

The very idea that events in the marketplace may affect the shape of the demand and supply curves seems incongruous to those who have been reared on classical economics. The demand and supply curves are supposed to determine the market price. If they were themselves subject to market influences, prices would cease to be uniquely determined. Instead of equilibrium, we would be left with fluctuating prices.

This would be a devastating state of affairs. All the conclusions of economic theory would lose their relevance to the real world. It is to prevent this outcome that the methodological device that treats the supply and demand curves as independently given was introduced. Yet there is something insidious about using a methodological device to obscure an assumption that would be untenable if it were spelled out.

Since my student days economists have gone to great lengths to fit the role of expectations into the theory of perfect competition. They developed the theory of rational expectations. I cannot pretend to fully understand the theory because I never studied it. If I understand it correctly, the theory asserts that market participants, in pursuing their self-interest, base their decisions on the assumption that the other participants will do the same. This sounds reasonable, but it is not, because participants act not on the basis of their best interests but on their *perception* of their best interests, and the two are not identical. This has been convincingly demonstrated by experiments in behavioral economics.[*] Market participants act on the basis of imperfect understanding, and their actions have unintended consequences. There is a lack of correspondence between expectations and outcomes—between *ex ante* and *ex post*—and it is not rational for people to act on the assumption that there is no divergence between the two.[†]

[*]Daniel Kahneman and Amos Tversky, "Prospect Theory: An Analysis of Decision under Risk," *Econometrica* (March 1979): 263–91.

[†]Roman Frydman and Michael D. Goldberg, *Imperfect Knowledge Economics: Exchange Rates and Risk* (Princeton: Princeton University Press, 2007); Roman Frydman and Edmund Phelps, *Individual Forecasting and Aggregate Outcomes: Rational Expectations Examined* (Cambridge: Cambridge University Press, 1983).

Rational expectations theory seeks to overcome this difficulty by claiming that the market as a whole always knows more than any individual participant—sufficiently so that markets manage to be always right. People may get things wrong, and misunderstandings may cause random disturbances; but in the ultimate analysis all market participants use the same model of how the world works, and when they do not, they learn from experience so that in the end they converge on the same model. I have considered this interpretation so far removed from reality that I did not even bother to study it. I have worked with a different model, and the fact that I have been successful using it makes nonsense out of rational expectations, because my performance far exceeds what would be a permissible deviation under the "random walk" theory.

A Contradictory Theory

I contend that financial markets are always wrong in the sense that they operate with a prevailing bias, but in the normal course of events they tend to correct their own excesses. Occasionally the prevailing bias can actually validate itself by influencing not only market prices but also the so-called fundamentals that market prices are supposed to reflect. That is the point that people steeped in the prevailing paradigm have such difficulty grasping. Many critics of reflexivity claimed that I was merely belaboring the obvious, namely that the participants' biased perceptions influence market prices. But the crux of the theory of reflexivity is not so obvious; it asserts that market prices can influence the fundamentals. The illusion that markets manage to be always right is caused by their ability to affect the fundamentals that they are supposed to reflect. The change in the fundamentals may then reinforce the biased expectations in an initially self-reinforcing but eventually self-defeating process. Of course such boom-bust sequences do not occur all the time. More often the prevailing bias corrects itself before it can affect the fundamentals. But the fact that they can occur invalidates the theory of rational expectations. When they occur, boom-bust processes can take on historic significance. That is what happened in the Great Depression, and that is what is unfolding now, although it is taking a very different shape.

In *The Alchemy of Finance* I cite many examples of boom-bust processes or bubbles from the financial markets. Each case involves a two-way, reflexive connection between market valuations and the so-called fundamentals that sets up some kind of short circuit between them whereby valuations affect the fundamentals that they are supposed to reflect. The short circuit may take the form of equity leveraging, that is, the issue of additional shares at inflated prices, but more commonly it involves the leveraging of debt. Most but not all cases involve real estate, commercial or residential, where the willingness to lend influences the value of the collateral. In the international banking crisis of the 1980s the short circuit occurred in sovereign borrowing; no collateral was involved, but the banks' willingness to lend affected the so-called debt ratios which determined the countries' ability to borrow.

THE CONGLOMERATE BOOM
OF THE 1960S

One of my early successes as a hedge fund manager was in exploiting the conglomerate boom that unfolded in the late 1960s. It started when the managements of some high-technology companies specializing in defense recognized that the prevailing growth rate their companies enjoyed could not be sustained in the aftermath of the Vietnam War. Companies such as Textron, LTV, and Teledyne started to use their relatively high-priced stock to acquire more mundane companies, and, as their per-share earnings growth accelerated, their price-earnings multiples, instead of contracting, expanded. They were the path breakers. The success of these companies attracted imitators; later on, even the most humdrum company could attain a higher multiple simply by going on an acquisition spree. Eventually, a company could achieve a higher multiple just by promising to put it to good use by making acquisitions.

Managements developed special accounting techniques that enhanced the beneficial impact of acquisitions. They also introduced changes in the acquired companies: They streamlined operations, disposed of assets, and generally focused on the bottom line, but these changes were less significant than the impact on per-share earnings of the acquisitions themselves.

Investors responded like pigs at the tough. At first, the record of each company was judged on its own merit, but gradually conglomerates became recognized as a group. A new breed of investors emerged: the early hedge fund managers, or gunslingers. They developed direct lines of communication with the managements of conglomerates, and conglomerates placed so-called letter stock directly with fund managers. The placement price was at a discount to the market price, but the stock could not be resold for a fixed period. Gradually, conglomerates learned to manage their stock prices as well as their earnings.

The misconception on which the conglomerate boom rested was the belief that companies should be valued according to the growth of their reported per-share earnings no matter how the growth was achieved. The misconception was exploited by managers who used their overvalued stock to buy companies on advantageous terms, thereby inflating the value of their stock even further. Analytically, the misconception could not have arisen if investors had understood reflexivity and realized that equity leveraging, that is, selling stock at inflated valuations, can generate earnings growth.

Multiples expanded, and eventually reality could not sustain expectations. More and more people became aware of the misconception on which the boom rested even as they continued to play the game. To maintain the momentum of earnings growth, acquisitions had to be larger and larger, and eventually conglomerates ran into the limits of size. The turning point came when Saul Steinberg of the Reliance Group sought to acquire Chemical Bank: It was fought and defeated by the white shoe establishment of the time.

When stock prices started to fall, the decline fed on itself. As the overvaluation diminished, it became impractical to make new acquisitions. The internal problems that had been swept under the carpet during the period of rapid external growth began to surface. Earnings reports revealed unpleasant surprises. Investors became disillusioned, and conglomerate managements went through their own crises: After the heady days of success, few were willing to buckle down to the drudgery of day-to-day management. As the president of one corporation told me: "I have no audience to play to." The situation was aggravated by a recession, and many of the high-flying conglomerates literally disintegrated. Investors were prepared to believe the worst, and for some companies the worst occurred. For others, reality turned out to be better than expectations, and eventually the situation stabilized. The surviving companies, often under new management, slowly worked themselves out from under the debris.

REAL ESTATE INVESTMENT TRUSTS

My best-documented encounter with a boom-bust sequence was that with real estate investment trusts, or REITs. REITs are a special corporate form brought into existence by legislation. Their key feature is that if they disburse more than 95 percent of their income, they can distribute it free of corporate taxation. The opportunity created by this legislation remained largely unexploited until 1969, when numerous mortgage trusts were founded. I was present at the creation, and, fresh from my experience with conglomerates, I recognized their boom-bust potential. I published a research report, where I argued that the conventional method of security analysis does not apply. Analysts try to predict the future course of earnings and then to estimate the price that investors may be willing to pay for those earnings. This method is inappropriate to mortgage trusts because the price that investors are willing to pay for the shares is an important factor in determining the future course of earnings. Instead of predicting future earnings and valuations separately, we should try to predict the future course of the entire initially self-reinforcing but eventually self-defeating process.

I then sketched out a drama in four acts. It starts with an overvaluation of the early mortgage trusts that allows them to justify the overvaluation by issuing additional shares at inflated prices; then come the imitators, who destroy the opportunity. The scenario ends in widespread bankruptcies.

My report had an interesting history. It came at a time when hedge fund managers had suffered severe losses in the collapse of the conglomerates. Since they were entitled to a share in the profits but they did not have to share in the losses, they were inclined to grasp at anything that held out the prospect of quickly recouping their losses. They instinctively understood how a reflexive process works because they had just participated in one, and they were eager to play again. The report found a tremendous response, the extent of which I realized only when I received a telephone call from a bank in Cleveland asking for a fresh copy of my report because theirs had gone through so many Xerox machines that it was no longer legible. There were only a few mortgage trusts in existence at the time, but the shares were so eagerly sought after that they nearly doubled in price in the space of a month or so. Demand generated supply, and a host of new issues came to market. When it became clear that the supply of new mortgage trusts was inexhaustible, prices fell almost as rapidly as they had risen. Obviously the readers of my report had failed to take into account the ease of entry, and their mistake was corrected in short order. Nevertheless, their initial enthusiasm helped to get the self-reinforcing process described in the report under way. Subsequent events took the course outlined in the report. Mortgage trusts enjoyed a boom that was not as violent as the one that came after the publication of my report, but it turned out to be more enduring.

I had invested heavily in mortgage trusts at the time I wrote my report and took some profits when the reception of my study exceeded my expectations. But I was sufficiently carried away by my own success to be caught holding an inventory of shares when the downdraft came. I hung on, and I even increased my positions. I continued to follow the industry closely for a year or so and eventually sold my holdings, realizing good profits. Then I lost touch with the group until a few years later when the problems began to surface. When I became aware of them I was tempted to establish short positions, but I was handicapped because I was no longer familiar with the companies. Nevertheless, when I reread the report I had written several years earlier, I found it so convincing that I decided to sell the group short more or less indiscriminately. Moreover as the shares fell I maintained the same level of exposure by selling additional shares short. My original prediction was fulfilled, and most mortgage trusts went broke. The result was that I reaped more than 100 percent profit on my short positions—a seeming impossibility since the maximum profit on a short position is 100 percent. (The explanation is that I kept on selling additional shares.)

THE INTERNATIONAL BANKING CRISIS
OF THE 1980s

All boom-bust processes contain an element of misunderstanding or misconception. In the two cases I have described, the process took the form of equity leveraging, that is, issuing shares at inflated prices, which was made possible by a misconception about earnings growth: Growth achieved by issuing additional shares at inflated prices was accorded the same premium as growth achieved by other means. Boom-bust processes, or bubbles, are more commonly associated with leveraging of debt rather than equity leveraging, but I analyzed only one instance in *The Alchemy of Finance*: the international banking crisis of the 1980s, which arose out of excessive lending to developing countries in the 1970s.

After the oil shock of 1973, caused by the formation of OPEC (Organization of the Petroleum Exporting Countries), the large money center banks were flooded with deposits from the oil producing countries, and they rechanneled them mainly to oil-importing countries that had to finance their balance of payments deficits. Banks used so-called debt ratios to evaluate the creditworthiness of the borrowing countries, but they failed to realize that the debt ratios were affected by their own lending activities, until it was too late.

In cases of debt leveraging the misconception consists in a failure to recognize a reflexive, two-way connection between the creditworthiness of the borrowers and the willingness of the creditors to lend: Usually there is a collateral involved, and the most common form of collateral is real estate. Bubbles arise when banks treat the value of the real estate as if it were independent of the banks' willingness to lend against it. The international banking crisis of the 1980s was somewhat different. The debtors were sovereign countries, and they pledged no collateral. Their creditworthiness was measured by the debt ratios, which turned out to be reflexive: Instead of being independently given, the debt ratios of borrowing countries were inflated during the 1970s by the banks' willingness to lend to them and an associated boom in commodity prices. The first country to run into severe difficulties was Mexico, which was an oil producing country. (Hungary preceded it but the problem was contained.) Since the international banking crisis of the 1980s I have witnessed several real estate bubbles in Japan, Britain, and the United States. The misconception can manifest itself in different guises, but the principle is always the same. What is amazing is that it keeps recurring.

THE BOOM-BUST MODEL

Using the conglomerate boom as my model, I devised a typical boom-bust sequence. The drama unfolds in eight stages. It starts with a prevailing bias and a prevailing trend. In the case of the conglomerate boom, the prevailing bias was a preference for rapid earnings growth per share without much attention to how it was brought about; the prevailing trend was the ability of companies to generate high earnings growth per share by using their stock to acquire other companies selling at a lower multiple of earnings. In the initial stage (1) the trend is not yet recognized. Then comes the period of acceleration (2), when the trend is recognized and reinforced by the prevailing bias. That is when the process approaches far-from-equilibrium territory. A period of testing (3) may intervene when prices suffer a setback. If the bias and trend survive the testing, both emerge stronger than ever, and far-from-equilibrium conditions, in which the normal rules no longer apply, become firmly established (4). Eventually there comes a moment of truth (5), when reality can no longer sustain the exaggerated expectations, followed by a twilight period (6), when people continue to play the game although they no longer believe in it. Eventually a crossover point (7) is reached, when the trend turns down and the bias is reversed, which leads to a catastrophic downward acceleration (8), commonly known as the crash.

THEORY

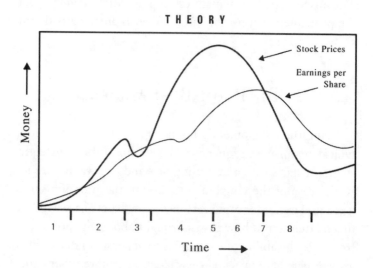

The boom-bust model I devised has a peculiarly asymmetric shape. It tends to start slowly, accelerate gradually and then fall steeper than it has risen. I have selected some real-life examples that resemble the prototype—although one of the graphs I am using here, LTV, is a little too symmetrical to serve as a good illustration.

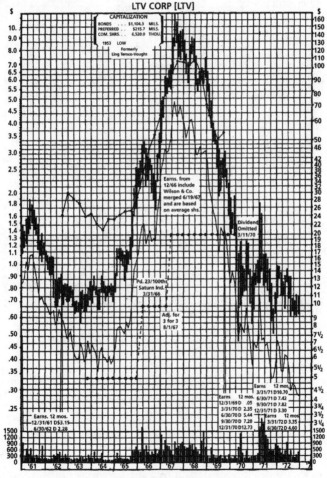

(Courtesy of Securities Research Company, a Division of
Babson-United Investment Advisors, Inc., 208 Newbury St., Boston, MA 02116.)

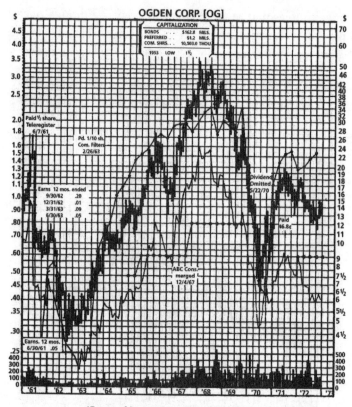

*(Courtesy of Securities Research Company, a Division of
Babson-United Investment Advisors, Inc., 208 Newbury St., Boston, MA 02116.)*

Exactly the same sequence could be observed in the international banking crisis. It followed the same asymmetric pattern—slow start, gradual acceleration in the boom phase, a moment of truth followed by a twilight period, and a catastrophic collapse. The reason I did not use it as my paradigm was that it did not lend itself to a graphic presentation. In the

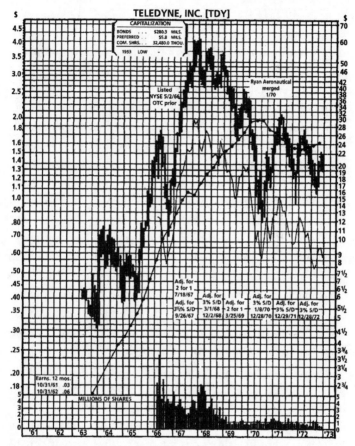

conglomerate boom, I could draw a chart showing stock
prices and earnings per share; in the international banking
crisis I could not create a similar graph.

OTHER FORMS OF REFLEXIVITY

It would be a mistake to think, however, that reflexive processes always manifest themselves in the form of a bubble. They can take many other forms. In freely floating exchange rate regimes, for instance, the reflexive relationship between market valuations and the so-called fundamentals tends to generate large multi-year waves. There is no difference between up and down, except in the case of runaway inflation, and there is no sign of the asymmetry that characterizes bubbles; there is even less evidence of a tendency towards equilibrium.

It is important to realize that two-way, reflexive connections are much more common in financial markets than boom-bust sequences. Market participants act on the basis of imperfect understanding at all times. Consequently market prices usually express a prevailing bias rather than the correct valuation. In the majority of cases, the valuations are proven wrong by subsequent evidence, and the bias is corrected, only to be replaced by a different bias. Only once in a blue moon does a prevailing bias set in motion an initially self-reinforcing but eventually self-defeating process. It happens only when the prevailing bias finds some kind of short circuit that allows it to affect the fundamentals. This is usually associated with a misunderstanding or misconception. Both market prices and economic conditions may then move far beyond anything that would be possible in the absence of a short circuit, and the correction, when it comes, may have catastrophic consequences.

MARKETS VERSUS REGULATORS

Because financial markets do not tend towards equilibrium they cannot be left to their own devices. Periodic crises bring forth regulatory reforms. That is how central banking and the regulation of financial markets have evolved. While boom-bust sequences occur only intermittently, the reflexive interplay between financial markets and the financial authorities is an ongoing process. The important thing to realize is that both market participants and financial authorities act on the basis of imperfect understanding; that is what makes the interaction between them reflexive.

Misunderstandings by either side usually stay within reasonable bounds because market prices provide useful information which allows both sides to recognize and correct their mistakes, but occasionally mistakes prove to be self-validating, setting in motion vicious or virtuous circles. Such circles resemble boom-bust processes in the sense that they are initially self-reinforcing but eventually self-defeating. Vicious and virtuous circles are few and far between, while reflexive interactions go on all the time. Reflexivity is a universal condition, while bubbles constitute a special case.

The distinguishing feature of reflexive processes is that they contain an element of uncertainty or indeterminacy. That uncertainty ensures that the behavior of financial markets is not determined by universally valid generalizations but follows a unique, irreversible path. Within that one-directional process we may distinguish between humdrum, everyday events, which are repetitive and lend themselves pretty well to statistical generalizations, and unique, historical events whose outcome is genuinely uncertain. Bubbles and other vicious or virtuous circles belong to the latter category. It should be realized, however, that reflexive, circular relationships do not necessarily generate historically significant processes. Those which are self-defeating to start with disappear without trace. Others are aborted along the way. Relatively few reach far-from-equilibrium territory. Moreover no process takes place in total isolation. Usually there are several reflexive processes going on at the same time, interfering with each other and producing irregular shapes. Regular patterns arise only on those rare occasions when a particular process is so powerful that it overshadows all the others. Perhaps I did not make this point sufficiently clear in *The Alchemy of Finance*.

THE FLAW IN EQUILIBRIUM THEORY

Equilibrium theory is not without merit. It provides a model with which reality can be compared. When I speak of far-from-equilibrium conditions I am also using the concept of equilibrium.* And economists have made many valiant attempts to adjust their models to take account of reality. So-called second-generation business cycle models have sought to analyze boom-bust situations. I cannot judge their validity,

---

*This could be easily misunderstood. Indeed it was misunderstood by one of my correspondents; hence this footnote. When I speak of far-from-equilibrium conditions, I am using "equilibrium" as a figure of speech. I do not mean to imply that there is a stable equilibrium from which a boom-bust process occasionally deviates. I think of equilibrium as a moving target because market prices can affect the fundamentals they are supposed to reflect.

but they certainly lack the simplicity of my boom-bust model. They remind me of pre-Copernican astronomers who sought to adjust their paradigm, which was circular, to the path followed by the planets, which is elliptical.

It is time for a new paradigm, and one is readily available in the theory of reflexivity—I mean the general theory, not just the boom-bust model. The theory cannot hope to gain scientific acceptance, however, without a fundamental reconsideration of what is to be expected from a theory dealing with social phenomena. If it has to meet the standards and criteria that apply to theories of natural science, the theory of reflexivity cannot possibly qualify because the theory asserts that there is a fundamental difference between the structure of natural and social events. If reflexivity introduces an element of indeterminacy into social events, then those events cannot possibly be predicted in a determinate fashion.

The prevailing paradigm asserts that financial markets tend towards equilibrium. That has led to the notion that actual prices deviate from a theoretical equilibrium in a random manner. While it is possible to construct theoretical models along those lines, the claim that those models apply to the real world is both false and misleading. It leaves out of account the possibility that the deviations may be self-reinforcing in the sense that they may alter the theoretical equilibrium. When that happens, risk calculation and trading techniques based on these models are liable to break down. In 1998 Long-Term Capital Management, a highly leveraged hedge fund employing such trading techniques and advised by two economists who got the Nobel Prize for devising the models, ran into trouble and had to be rescued with the help of the New York Federal Reserve. The techniques and models were modified, but the basic approach was not abandoned. It was observed that price deviations did not follow the normal shape of a bell curve, but had a thick tail. To allow for the extra risk posed by this phenomenon, stress tests were introduced to supplement value-at-risk calculations. But the reason for the thick tails was left unexplained. The reason is to be found in self-reinforcing price movements; but reflexivity continued to be ignored, and the use of mistaken models—particularly in the design of synthetic financial instruments—continued to spread. This is at the root of the current financial crisis, which will be discussed in Part 2.

Renouncing the Unity of Method

The belief that markets tend towards equilibrium has given rise to policies which seek to give financial markets free rein. I call these policies market fundamentalism, and I contend that market fundamentalism is no better than Marxist dogma. Both ideologies cloak themselves in scientific guise in order to make themselves more acceptable, but the theories they invoke do not stand up to the test of reality. They use scientific method to manipulate reality, not to understand it. The fact that scientific method can be used in such a way should be a warning sign that there is something wrong with applying the same methods and criteria to both natural and social science. As I have shown in my discussion of the human uncertainty principle, social situations can be influenced by making statements about them. In other words, they can be manipulated. One of Karl Popper's contributions was to show that ideologies like Marxism do not qualify as scientific. But he did not go far enough. He did not recognize that mainstream economics can also be exploited in the same nonscientific way. The fault lies with the doctrine of the unity of method. By endowing social science with the prestige of natural science it allows scientific theories to be used for manipulative rather than cognitive purposes.

The trap can be avoided, however. All we have to do is renounce the doctrine and adopt the theory of reflexivity. There is a heavy price to pay: Economists have to accept a reduction in their status. No wonder that they put up resistance. But if the objective is to pursue the cognitive function, the price is well worth paying. Not only does the theory of reflexivity provide a better explanation of how financial markets function, but it is also less conducive to the manipulation of reality than the currently prevailing scientific theories because it avoids making excessive claims about its ability to predict and explain social phenomena. Once we recognize that reality can be manipulated, our first priority ought to be to prevent the manipulative function from interfering with the pursuit of knowledge. The theory of reflexivity serves that purpose well by proclaiming that social events become unpredictable whenever reflexivity makes it presence felt. Accordingly we must reduce our expectations for the social sciences. We cannot expect reflexive events to be determined according to timelessly valid generalizations when reflexivity contains an element of uncertainty and indeterminacy (uncertainty relates to the participants' thinking, indeterminacy to the course of events).

One possible objection to abandoning the doctrine of the unity of method is that it is impossible to draw a hard and fast dividing line between the natural and social sciences. But if we follow this line of argument we need not be bothered by the fact that the dividing line between the natural and social sciences is a fuzzy one. Whenever reflexivity rears its ugly head we must reduce our expectations.

THE NEW PARADIGM

Let me now spell out how the new paradigm differs from the old one as regards the financial markets. Instead of being always right, financial markets are always wrong. They have the ability, however, both to correct themselves and occasionally to make their mistakes come true by a reflexive process of self-validation. That is how they can appear to be always right. To be specific, financial markets cannot predict economic downturns accurately, but they can cause them.

Participants act on the basis of imperfect understanding. They base their decisions on incomplete, biased, and misconceived interpretations of reality, not on knowledge, and the outcomes are liable to diverge from expectations. The divergence provides useful feedback on the basis of which they can adjust their behavior. Such a process is unlikely to produce satisfactory results all the time. Indeed markets move away from a theoretical equilibrium almost as often as they move towards it, and they can get caught up in initially self-reinforcing but eventually self-defeating processes. Bubbles often lead to financial crises. Crises, in turn, lead to the regulation of financial markets. That is how the financial system has evolved—periodic crises leading to regulatory reforms. That is why financial markets are best interpreted as a historical process, and that is why that process cannot be understood without taking into account the role of the regulators. In the absence of regulatory authorities, financial markets would be bound to break down, but in reality breakdowns rarely occur because markets operate under constant supervision, and even if the authorities tend to be sluggish in normal times, they become alert in an emergency—at least in democracies.

Most of the reflexive processes involve an interplay between market participants and regulators. To understand that interplay it is important to remember that the regulators are just as fallible as the participants. Changes in the regulatory environment place every crisis into a unique historical context. That alone is sufficient to justify my claim that the behavior of markets is best regarded as a historical process.

Market fundamentalists blame market failures on the fallibility of the regulators, and they are half right: Both markets and regulators are fallible. Where market fundamentalists are totally wrong is in claiming that regulations ought to be abolished on account of their fallibility. That happens to be the inverse of the Communist claim that markets ought to be abolished on account of their fallibility. Karl Popper (and Friedrich Hayek) have demonstrated the dangers of the Communist ideology. It will advance our understanding of reality if we recognize the ideological character of market fundamentalism. The fact that regulators are fallible does not prove that markets are perfect. It merely justifies reexamining and improving the regulatory environment.

When do the reflexive connections which are endemic in financial markets turn into self-reinforcing, historically significant processes which affect not only prices in the financial markets but also the so-called fundamentals that those prices are supposed to reflect? That is the question that a theory of reflexivity has to answer if it is to be of any value. The subject deserves more detailed investigation, but based on theoretical arguments and empirical evidence, my preliminary hypothesis is that *there has to be both some form of credit or leverage and some kind of misconception or misinterpretation involved for a boom-bust process to develop.* That is the hypothesis I am now submitting for testing. As I said before, the main insight my conceptual framework has to offer is that misconceptions play a significant role in the making of history. This message is particularly relevant to understanding what is happening in the financial markets at the present moment in history.

One of the major differences between the new paradigm and the old one is that the new one takes a more cautionary approach to the use of leverage. The theory of reflexivity recognizes the uncertainties associated with the fallibility of both regulators and market participants. The prevailing paradigm acknowledges only known risks and fails to allow for the consequences of its own deficiencies and misconceptions. That lies at the root of the current turmoil.

PART II

The Current Crisis and Beyond

CHAPTER 5

The Super-Bubble Hypothesis

We are in the midst of a financial crisis the likes of which has not been seen since the Great Depression of the 1930s. To be sure, it is not the prelude to another Great Depression. History does not repeat itself. The banking system will not be allowed to collapse as it did in 1932 exactly because its collapse then caused the Great Depression. At the same time, the current crisis is not comparable to the periodic crises which have afflicted particular segments of the financial system since the 1980s—the international banking crisis of 1982, the savings and loan crisis of 1986, the portfolio insurance debacle of 1987, the failure of Kidder Peabody in 1994, the emerging market crisis of 1997, the failure of Long Term Capital Management in 1998, the technology bubble of 2000. This crisis is not confined to a particular firm or a particular segment of the financial system; it has brought the entire system to the brink of a breakdown, and it is being contained only with the greatest difficulty. This will have far-reaching consequences. It is not business as usual but the end of an era.

To explain what I mean by this somewhat bombastic statement, I shall have recourse to the theory of reflexivity and the boom-bust model I introduced in chapter 4, but the explanation I shall provide will be far from simple. There is not just one boom-bust process or bubble to consider but two: the housing bubble and what I shall call a longer-term super-bubble. The housing bubble is quite straightforward; the super-bubble is much more complicated. To further complicate matters the two bubbles did not develop in isolation; they are deeply imbedded in the history of the period. In particular, the current situation cannot be understood without taking into account the economic strength of China, India, and some oil- and raw material–producing countries; the commodities boom; an exchange rate system that is partly floating, partly tied to the dollar and partly in between; and the increasing unwillingness of the rest of the world to hold dollars.

The U.S. Housing Bubble

In the aftermath of the technology bubble that burst in 2000 and the terrorist attack of September 11, 2001, the Federal Reserve lowered the federal funds rate to 1 percent and kept it there until June 2004. This allowed a housing bubble to develop in the United States. Similar bubbles could be observed in other parts of the world, notably the United Kingdom, Spain, and Australia. What sets the United States housing bubble apart from the others is its size and importance for the global economy and the international financial system. The housing market turned down earlier in Spain than in the United States, but that passed unnoticed, except locally. By contrast, U.S. mortgage securities have been widely distributed all over the world with some European, particularly German, institutional holders even more heavily involved than American ones.

Taken on its own the United States housing bubble faithfully followed the course prescribed for it by my boom-bust model. There was a prevailing trend—ever more aggressive relaxation of lending standards and expansion of loan-to-value ratios—and it was supported by a prevailing misconception that the value of the collateral was not affected by the willingness to lend. That is the most common misconception that has fueled bubbles in the past, particularly in the real estate area. What is amazing is that the lesson has still not been learned.

The growth of the bubble can be vividly illustrated by a few charts. In Chart 1, the declining line shows the savings rate (right scale), the rising one, house prices adjusted for inflation. Chart 2 shows the unprecedented increase in mortgage debt. Americans have added more household mortgage debt in the last six years than in the prior life of the mortgage market. Chart 3 shows the decline in credit quality. Since the rating agencies based their valuations on past loss experience, and loss experience improved during rising house prices, the rating agencies became increasingly generous in the valuations of collateralized mortgage obligations. At the same time, mortgage originators became increasingly aggressive in their residential lending practices (which is not picked up in this chart). Towards the end, houses could be bought with no money down, no questions asked. The 2005 and 2006 vintage subprime and Alt-A mortgages are of notoriously low quality. Chart 4 shows the growing share of subprime and Alt-A originations. In 2006, 33 percent of all mortgage originations fell into these two categories. Charts 3 and 4 together indicate the deterioration in credit quality. The process was driven by the pursuit of fee income. Chart 5 shows the rise of Moody's revenues from the rating of structured products. By 2006, Moody's revenues from structured products were on par with revenues from its traditional bond rating business. Chart 6 shows the exponential growth of synthetic products.

The bubble started slowly, lasted for several years, and did not reverse itself immediately when interest rates started rising, because it was sustained by speculative demand, aided and abetted by ever more aggressive lending practices and ever more sophisticated ways of securitizing mortgages. Eventually the moment of truth arrived in the spring of 2007, when the subprime problem pushed New Century Financial Corporation into bankruptcy, which was followed by a twilight period when housing prices were falling but people failed to realize that the game was over. The chief executive officer of Citibank, Chuck Prince, was reported saying that "When the music stops, in terms of liquidity, things will be complicated. But as long as the music is playing, you've got to get up and dance. We're still dancing."* When the crossover point was finally reached, in August 2007, there was a catastrophic acceleration on the downside aggravated by a contagion that spread from one segment of the market to another. That was reminiscent of the wrecking ball that knocked down one country after another in the emerging

---

*Michiyo Nakamoto and David Wighton, "Bullish Citigroup Is 'Still Dancing' to the Beat of the Buy-Out Boom," *Financial Times*, July 10, 2007.

Chart 1: U.S. Personal Saving Rate

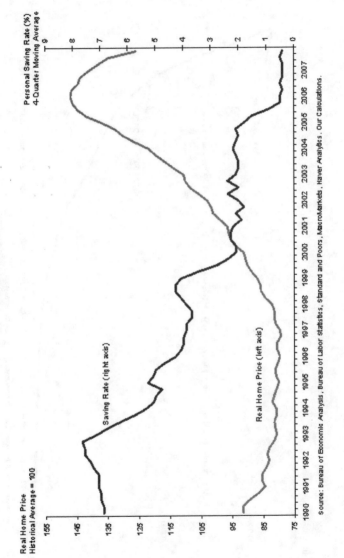

Real Home Price
Historical Average = 100

Personal Saving Rate (%)
4-Quarter Moving Average

Saving Rate (right axis)

Real Home Price (left axis)

Source: Bureau of Economic Analysis, Bureau of Labor Statistics, Standard and Poors, MacroMarkets, Haver Analytics. Our Calculations.

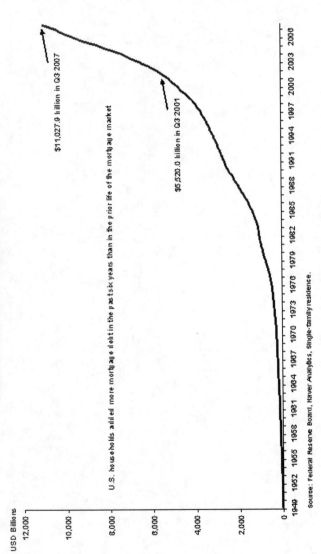

Chart 2: Growth in U.S. Household Mortgage Debt

USD Billions

$11,027.9 billion in Q3 2007

U.S. households added more mortgage debt in the past six years than in the prior life of the mortgage market

$5,520.0 billion in Q3 2001

Source: Federal Reserve Board, Haver Analytics, Single-family residence.

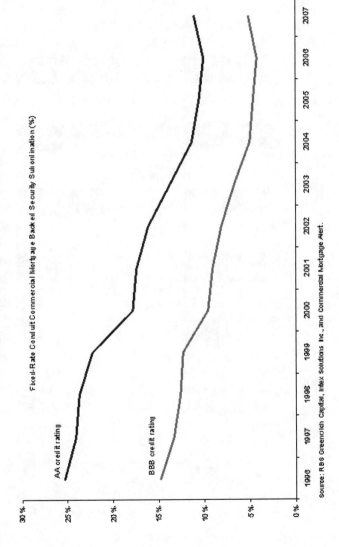

Chart 3: Real Estate Lending Has Been Safer and Safer?

Fixed-Rate Conduit Commercial Mortgage-Backed Security Subordination (%)

AA credit rating

BBB credit rating

Source: RBS Greenwich Capital, Intex Solutions Inc., and Commercial Mortgage Alert.

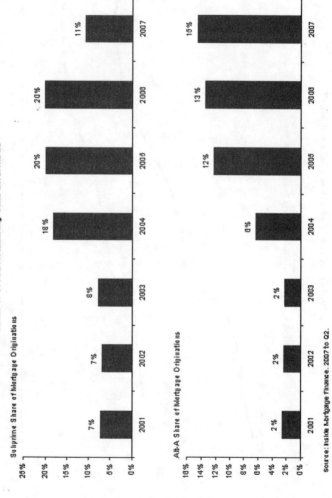

Chart 4: Credit Availability Was Enormous

Subprime Share of Mortgage Originations

2001	2002	2003	2004	2005	2006	2007
7%	7%	8%	18%	20%	20%	11%

Alt-A Share of Mortgage Originations

2001	2002	2003	2004	2005	2006	2007
2%	2%	2%	6%	12%	13%	15%

Source: Inside Mortgage Finance. 2007 to Q2.

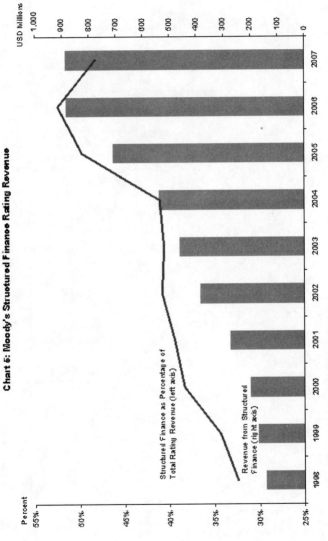

Chart 6: Moody's Structured Finance Rating Revenue

USD Millions

Percent

Structured Finance as Percentage of Total Rating Revenue (left axis)

Revenue from Structured Finance (right axis)

Source: Moody's Annual Reports 2000-2007. Our Calculations.

90

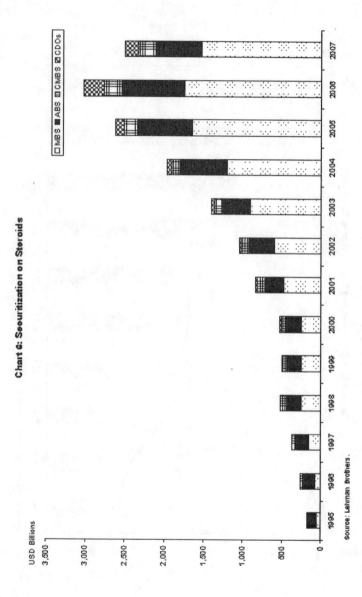

Chart 6: Securitization on Steroids

USD Billions

Source: Lehman Brothers.

market crisis of 1997. Even so, the stock market recovered from August 2007 to October of that year. That move was not anticipated by my model. The model calls for a collapse that is short and sharp and is followed by a slow and laborious return to near-equilibrium conditions. In this case there was an incomplete give-up in August 2007 and another in January 2008. On each occasion the Fed intervened and lowered the federal funds rate, and the stock market took heart in the belief that the Fed will protect the economy from the consequences of the financial crisis as it has done in the past. I consider that belief misplaced. The Fed is constrained in its ability to protect the economy by the fact that it has done it too often. In my view, this financial crisis is not like the others which have occurred in recent history.

THE SUPER-BUBBLE HYPOTHESIS

Superimposed on the U.S. housing bubble there is a much larger boom-bust sequence which has finally reached its inflection, or crossover, point. The super-bubble is more complex than the housing bubble and requires a more complicated explanation. Boom-bust processes arise out of a reflexive interaction between a prevailing trend and a prevailing misconception. The prevailing trend in the super-bubble is the same as in the housing bubble—ever more sophisticated methods of credit creation—but the misconception is different. It consists of an excessive reliance on the market mechanism. President Ronald Reagan called it the magic of the marketplace. I call it market fundamentalism. It became the dominant creed in 1980 when Reagan became president in the United States and Margaret Thatcher prime minister in the United Kingdom, although its antecedents go back much further. It was called *laissez-faire* in the nineteenth century.

Market fundamentalism has its roots in the theory of perfect competition, as it was originally propounded by Adam Smith and developed by the classical economists. In the post World War II period it received a powerful fillip from the failures of communism, socialism, and other forms of state intervention. That impetus, however, rests on false premises. The fact that state intervention is always flawed does not make markets perfect. The cardinal contention of the theory of reflexivity is that all human constructs are flawed. Financial markets do not necessarily tend towards equilibrium; left to their own devices they are liable to go to extremes of euphoria and despair. For that reason they are not left to their own devices; they have been put in the charge of financial authorities whose job it is to supervise them and regulate them. Ever since the Great Depression, the authorities have been remarkably successful in avoiding any major breakdown in the international financial system. Ironically, it is their success that has allowed market fundamentalism to revive. When I studied at the London School of Economics in the 1950s, *laissez-faire* seemed to have been buried for good. Yet it came back in the 1980s. Under its influence the financial authorities lost control of financial markets and the super-bubble developed.

The super-bubble combines three major trends, each containing at least one defect. First is the long-term trend towards ever increasing credit expansion as indicated by rising loan-to-value ratios in housing and consumer loans, and rising volume of credit to gross national product ratios (see Chart 7). This trend is the result of the countercyclical policies developed in response to the Great Depression. Every time the banking system is endangered, or a recession looms, the financial authorities intervene, bailing out the endangered institutions and stimulating the economy. Their intervention introduces an asymmetric incentive for credit expansion also known as the moral hazard. The second trend is the globalization of financial markets, and the third is the progressive removal of financial regulations and the accelerating pace of financial innovations. As we shall see, globalization also has an asymmetric structure. It favors the United States and other developed countries at the center of the financial system and penalizes the less-developed economies at the periphery. The disparity between the center and the periphery is not widely recognized, but it has played an important role in the development of the super-bubble. And, as I have already mentioned, both deregulation and many of the recent innovations were based on the false assumption that markets tend towards equilibrium and deviations are random.

The super-bubble ties together the three trends and the three defects. The first trend can be traced back to the 1930s, but the second and third became firmly established only in the 1980s. So one can date the inception of the super-bubble to the 1980s because that is when market fundamentalism became the guiding principle of the international financial system. Clearly, the super-bubble is not a simple process to trace or to explain.

GLOBALIZATION

The globalization of financial markets was a very successful market fundamentalist project. If financial capital is free to move about, it becomes difficult for any state to tax it or to regulate it because it can move somewhere else. This puts financial capital into a privileged position. Governments often have to pay more heed to the requirements of international capital than to the aspirations of their own people. That is why the globalization of financial markets served the objectives of the market fundamentalists so well. The process started with the recycling of petro-dollars in the aftermath of the 1973 oil shock, but it accelerated during the Reagan-Thatcher years.

Globalization did not bring about the level playing field that free markets were supposed to provide according to the market fundamentalist doctrine. The international financial system is under the control of a consortium of financial authorities representing the developed countries. They constitute the Washington consensus. They seek to impose strict market discipline on individual countries, but they are willing to bend the rules when the financial system itself is endangered. The way the system works, the United States, which enjoys veto power in the Bretton Woods institutions—the International Monetary Fund and the World Bank—is "more equal" than others. The dollar has served as the main international reserve currency readily accepted by the central banks of the world. Consequently the United States has been able to pursue countercyclical policies while the developing countries, and to a lesser extent other developed countries, were obliged to live within their means. This has made it safer to hold financial assets at the center than at the periphery. As the barriers to capital movements were removed the savings of the world were sucked up to the center and redistributed from there. In a not-so-strange coincidence, the United States developed a chronic current account deficit in the Reagan years. The deficit has continued to grow ever since, and it reached 6.6 percent of GDP in the third quarter of 2006. The American consumer became the motor of the world economy.

LIBERALIZATION

At the end of World War II the financial industry—banks and markets—were strictly regulated. The postwar years saw the gradual lifting of restrictions, slowly at first, gradually accelerating, and reaching a crescendo in the 1980s. Since financial markets do not tend towards equilibrium, their liberalization gave rise to occasional crises. Most of the crises occurred in the less developed world and could be ascribed to their lack of development, but some endangered the stability of the international financial system, notably the international banking crisis of the 1980s and the emerging market crisis of 1997–1998. In these cases the financial authorities were willing to bend the rules to save the system, but market discipline continued to apply to the less developed world.

This asymmetry, combined with the asymmetric incentive for credit expansion in the developed world, sucked up the savings of the world from the periphery to the center and allowed the United States to develop a chronic current account deficit. Starting in the Reagan years, the United States also developed a large budget deficit. Paradoxically the budget deficit helped to finance the current account deficit because the surplus countries invested their swelling monetary reserves in United States government and agency bonds. This was a perverse situation because capital was flowing from the less-developed world to the United States and both the current account and the budget deficits of the United States served as major sources of credit expansion. Another major source was the introduction of new financial instruments and the increased use of leverage by the banks and some of their customers, notably hedge funds and private equity funds. Yet another source of credit expansion was Japan, which, in the aftermath of a real estate bubble, lowered interest rates to practically zero and is keeping them there indefinitely. This gave rise to the so-called carry trade, whereby foreign institutions borrowed yen, and Japanese individuals used their savings to invest in higher yielding currencies, often on a leveraged basis.

These imbalances could have continued to grow indefinitely because willing lenders and willing borrowers were well matched. There was a symbiotic relationship between the United States, which was happy to consume more than it produced, and China and other Asian exporters, which were happy to produce more than they consumed. The United States accumulated external debt; China and the others accumulated currency reserves. The United States had low savings rates, the others high ones. There was a similar symbiotic relationship between banks and their customers, especially hedge funds and private equity funds, and also between mortgage lenders and borrowers.

The situation became unsustainable with the development of a housing bubble in the U.S. and the introduction of financial innovations based on a false paradigm. Synthetic financial instruments, risk calculations, and propriatary trading models built on the theory that markets tend toward equilibrium and deviations are random. They took past experience as their starting point, with suitable allowances for deviation and emerging new trends, but they failed to recognize the impact that they, themselves, made. Households became increasingly dependent on the double-digit appreciation in house prices. The savings rate dropped below zero, and households withdrew equity by refinancing their mortgages at an ever increasing rate. Mortgage equity withdrawals reached nearly a trillion dollars in 2006. This was 8 percent of the GDP at its peak, or more than the current account deficit. When house prices stopped rising these trends had to moderate and eventually reverse. Households found themselves overexposed and overindebted. Eventually, consumption had to fall. The bust is following the classic boom-bust pattern, but, in addition, it has also set in motion a flight from the dollar and an unwinding of the other excesses introduced into the financial system by recent innovations. That is how the housing bubble and the super-bubble are connected.

To properly understand what is happening, it is important to realize the difference between this crisis and the periodic crises that have punctuated financial history since the 1980s. The previous crises served as successful tests which reinforced both the prevailing trend and the prevailing misconception of the long-term super-bubble. The current crisis plays a different role: It constitutes the inflection, or crossover, point not only in the housing bubble but also in the long term super-bubble. Those who kept insisting that the subprime crisis was an isolated phenomenon lacked a proper understanding of the situation. The subprime crisis was merely the trigger that released the unwinding of the super-bubble.

While it is clear, in retrospect, that the previous crises played the role of successful tests that reinforced the super-bubble, the role and significance of the current crisis is less clearly defined. My contention that it constitutes the end of an era is just that—a contention, not a fact or a scientific prediction. It needs to be substantiated.

There is considerable evidence to support the super-bubble hypothesis. Credit conditions have been relaxed to such an extent that it is difficult to see how they could be relaxed any further. This is certainly true as far as the U.S. consumer is concerned. Credit terms for mortgages, auto loans, and credit cards have reached their maximum extension. The same is true for some other developed countries, like the United Kingdom and Australia. It may also be true for commercial credit, particularly for leveraged buyouts and commercial real estate. But the same argument could also have been made in connection with previous financial crises. Indeed, I made that argument in *The Crisis of Global Capitalism* at the time of the emerging market crisis of 1997, and I was proven wrong. One cannot predict what new methods of credit creation may be invented and what new sources of funds may be discovered. For instance, in the current crisis a few banks were able to replenish their capital from sovereign wealth funds. Similarly, after the 1987 stock market debacle, Japan emerged as the lender and investor of last resort. In case of need, the Federal Reserve can always print more dollars. So the argument that we have run out of new sources of funds is not fully convincing.

More persuasive is the evidence that this time the crisis is not confined to a particular segment of financial markets but has enveloped the entire financial system. With every passing day it becomes more evident that the current crisis cannot pass as a successful test. The unraveling of markets has defied the efforts of the financial authorities to bring them under control. The central banks have succeeded in pumping liquidity into the banking system, but the flow of credit from the banks to the economy has been disrupted more severely and for a longer period than on any previous occasion. This is the first time since the Great Depression that the international financial system has come close to a genuine meltdown. That is the crucial difference between this financial crisis and previous ones.

What is it that sets the current crisis apart from previous ones? The central banks play the same countercyclical role as before. They were slow to react on this occasion, partly because they may have genuinely believed that the subprime crisis was an isolated phenomenon and partly because they were concerned about the moral hazard. One way or another, they fell behind the curve. But once it became clear that the disruption of the financial sector was going to affect the real economy, the authorities were ready, as always, to provide monetary and fiscal stimulus. Their ability to stimulate the economy is constrained by three factors: First, financial innovation has run amok in recent years, and some of the recently introduced markets and financial instruments have proven unsound and are now unraveling. Second, the willingness of the rest of the world to hold dollars is impaired.

This limits the capacity of the financial authorities to engage in countercyclical policies because these policies could set off a flight from the dollar and raise the specter of runaway inflation. The United States finds itself in a position reminiscent of countries at the periphery. In other words, some of the advantages of being in undisputed control of the system have been lost. Third, the capital base of the banks is severely impaired, and they are unable to get a good grip on their risk exposure. Their first priority is to reduce their exposure. As a result they are unwilling and unable to pass on to their customers the monetary stimulus provided by the Fed. These three factors render an economic slowdown virtually inevitable and turn what should have been a successful test into the end of an era.

The three factors I have identified are closely connected with the three defects which allowed the super-bubble to develop. They are what give the super-bubble its exceptional power. But we must beware of laying too much emphasis on the super-bubble. We must not endow it with magical powers the way President Reagan did with the marketplace. There is nothing predetermined or compulsory about the boom-bust pattern. It is just one manifestation of the reflexive relationships that characterize financial markets, and it does not occur in isolation. Occasionally the pattern becomes so pronounced that it can be studied as if it were an isolated phenomenon. That is the case with the housing bubble, but even there the introduction of synthetic instruments like CDOs (collateralized debt obligations), CDO^2s, and tradable indexes changed the course of events. The super-bubble, as we have seen, is more complicated because it contains other bubbles and the influence of many other factors. I have already mentioned some of them in passing: the commodity boom, the rise of China, etc. I shall deal with them in greater detail when I try to reconstruct the history of the super-bubble. Here I want to caution against the pitfalls that await those who seek to fit the course of events into a predetermined pattern; they are liable to leave many other important factors out of account. The right way to proceed is to fit the pattern to the actual course of events. That is how I arrived at the idea of a super-bubble.

REFLEXIVITY

When I speak of a new paradigm, I do not have the boom-bust pattern in mind; I am referring to the theory of reflexivity. The boom-bust pattern is merely a convincing example of reflexivity. It is convincing because it describes market behavior that is in direct contradiction with the prevailing paradigm, which holds that markets tend towards equilibrium. It ought to be particularly persuasive at the present time, when the markets are in turmoil. The prevailing paradigm cannot explain what is happening; the theory of reflexivity can. The case for abandoning the prevailing paradigm is even stronger: The belief that markets tend towards equilibrium is directly responsible for the current turmoil; it encouraged the regulators to abandon their responsibility and rely on the market mechanism to correct its own excesses. The idea that prices, although they may take random walks, tend to revert to the mean served as the guiding principle for the synthetic financial instruments and investment practices which are currently unraveling.

The theory of reflexivity is different in character from equilibrium theory. Equilibrium theory claims to be a scientific theory in accordance with Karl Popper's model of scientific method. It offers universally valid generalizations that can be used reversibly to provide determinate predictions and explanations similar to the theories of natural science. The theory of reflexivity makes no such claim. It contends that reflexivity, whenever it occurs, introduces an element of indeterminacy into the course of events; therefore it would be inappropriate to look for theories that provide determinate predictions.

I believe that the theory of reflexivity can explain the current states of affairs better than the prevailing paradigm, but I have to admit that it cannot do what the old paradigm did. It cannot offer generalizations in the mold of natural science. It contends that social events are fundamentally different from natural phenomena; they have thinking participants whose biased views and misconceptions introduce an element of uncertainty into the course of events. Consequently the course of events follows a one-directional path that is not determined in advance by universally valid laws, but emerges out of the reflexive interplay between the participants' views and the actual state of affairs. Accordingly the theory of reflexivity can explain events with greater certainty than it can predict the future. That is very different from what we have come to expect from scientific theories. Accordingly, the theory of reflexivity requires a far-reaching revision of the way social scientists in general and economists in particular interpret the world. That is what has stood in the way of reflexivity becoming the generally accepted paradigm. The severity of the current financial crisis may facilitate a breakthrough.

My theory has been out there for twenty years, but it has not been taken seriously. Even I had doubts about its significance. Admittedly I was not precise and consistent enough in my exposition, and even now I could probably do better. But I no longer have any doubt that the paradigm I am proposing can explain the current state of affairs better than the prevailing one. How far the new paradigm can be developed remains to be seen. There is just so much that one person can do on his own. Others need to get engaged. That is what has prompted me to write this book.

According to the new paradigm, events in financial markets are best interpreted as a form of history. The past is uniquely determined, the future is uncertain. Consequently it is easier to explain how the present position has been reached than it is to predict where it will lead. Currently not one but several reflexive processes are at work at the same time; that renders the range of possibilities exceptionally wide. But explanations also run into difficulties. History, although it is uniquely determined, is so overcrowded that it would be incomprehensible unless the processes and singular events involved were reduced to manageable numbers. That is where the super-bubble hypothesis can be useful. In studying history a hypothesis can help to select the events and developments that deserve consideration.

The super-bubble hypothesis could be used to create a comprehensive financial history of the post–World War II period, culminating in the current crisis. But that is beyond the scope of this book, and my capacity. In the next chapter, however, I substitute for it my experience in the financial markets over the past fifty-five years—a personal history of the time. I think it may be more illuminating than a detailed historical account. After that, I turn to the problem of projecting that experience forward. I record both my outlook at the start of this year and subsequent changes in my views. This real-time experiment is designed to shed light on how my approach works in practice. Following that, I begin a discussion of possible policy responses.

CHAPTER 6

Autobiography of
a Successful Speculator

One of the advantages of having been engaged in the financial markets for more than fifty years is that I have a personal memory of their evolution. In the course of my career I have seen them change out of all recognition. Arrangements that would be outlandish today were at one time accepted as natural, or even unavoidable. And vice versa. Financial instruments and financing techniques that are in widespread use today would have been inconceivable in earlier times. I remember the time when I was an arbitrage trader specializing in warrants and convertible bonds. I was dreaming of creating tradable warrants out of stocks, but of course that would not have been allowed by the regulators. I could not have imagined the range of synthetic instruments that are regularly traded today.

At the end of World War II, the financial industry—banks, brokers, other financial institutions—played a very different role in the economy than they do today. Banks and markets were strictly regulated. The total amount of credit outstanding in relation to the size of the economy was much less than it is today, and the amounts that could be borrowed against different types of collateral were also much smaller. Mortgages required at least 20 percent down payment, and borrowings against stocks were subject to statutory margin requirements that restricted loans to 50 percent or less of the value of the collateral. Auto loans, which required down payment, have been largely replaced by leases, which do not. There were no credit cards and very little unsecured credit. Financial institutions represented only a small percentage of the market capitalization of U.S. stocks. Very few financial stocks were listed on the New York Stock Exchange. Most banks were traded over the counter, and many of them traded only by appointment.

International financial transactions were subject to strict regulation by most countries, and there was very little international capital movement. The Bretton Woods institutions were set up in order to facilitate international trade and to make up for the lack of international investment by the private sector. They were brought into existence by the United States in consultation with a British delegation led by John Maynard Keynes. The British proposed and the United States disposed. The shareholders of the Bretton Woods institutions were the governments of the developed world, but the United States retained veto rights.

Although the international financial system was officially on the gold standard, in effect the dollar served as the international currency. The price of gold was fixed in dollars. For a while the countries of the British Commonwealth remained tied to sterling, but as sterling kept depreciating, the sterling area gradually disintegrated. In the aftermath of the war there was an acute shortage of dollars, and the United States embarked on the Marshall Plan to facilitate the rebuilding of Europe. Gradually the dollar shortage was relieved, and with the formation of the European Common Market and the resurgence of Japan—to be imitated by the Asian tigers—the situation was reversed. Large-scale capital outflows, trade deficits, and the Vietnam War combined to bring the dollar under pressure. But control of the international financial system remained firmly in the hands of the developed countries, with the United States in a dominant position. When the convertibility of the dollar into gold was suspended on August 15, 1971, the dollar remained the main currency in which central banks kept their reserves.

I started my career as a trainee in a London merchant bank in 1953 or 1954, and learned arbitrage trading in stocks. Arbitrage means trying to take advantage of slight price differences between different markets. International trading at the time was mainly confined to oil and gold stocks, and it required the use of a special type of currency known as switch sterling, or premium dollars. Official exchange rates were fixed, but the currencies used for capital transactions fluctuated beyond the official band according to supply and demand.

I moved to the United States in 1956. After the formation of the European Common Market, there was a lively interest in investing in European securities, and I became actively involved as a trader, security analyst, and salesman. The business came to an abrupt end in 1963 when President John F. Kennedy introduced a so-called interest equalization tax, which effectively imposed a 15 percent surcharge on the purchase of foreign securities abroad. Gradually I shifted my attention to U.S. securities, first as an analyst and then as a hedge fund manager. I belong to the first generation of hedge fund managers. There was not more than a handful of us when I started.

As an analyst I witnessed the gradual awakening of the banking industry. In 1972 I wrote a report entitled "The Case for Growth Banks." Banks at the time were considered the stodgiest of institutions. Managements had been traumatized by the failures of the 1930s, and safety was the paramount consideration, overshadowing profit or growth. The structure of the industry was practically frozen by regulation. Expansion across state lines was prohibited, and in some states even branch banking was outlawed. A dull business attracted dull people, and there was little movement or innovation in the industry. Bank stocks were ignored by investors looking for capital gains.

In my report I argued that conditions were changing, but the changes were not recognized by investors. A new breed of bankers was emerging who had been educated in business schools and thought in terms of bottom-line profits. The spiritual center of the new school of thinking was First National City Bank under the leadership of Walter Wriston, and people trained there were fanning out and occupying top spots at other banks. New kinds of financial instruments were being introduced, and some banks were beginning to utilize their capital more aggressively and putting together very creditable earnings performances. The better banks showed a return on equity in excess of 13 percent. In any other industry, such a return on equity, combined with per-share earnings growth of better than 10 percent, would have been rewarded by the shares selling at a decent premium over asset value, but bank shares were selling at little or no premium. Yet many banks had reached the point where they were pushing against the limits of what was considered prudent leverage by the standards of the time. If they wanted to continue growing they would need to raise additional equity capital. It was against this background that First National City hosted a dinner for security analysts—an unheard-of event in the banking industry.

That is what prompted me to publish my report in which I argued that bank stocks were about to come alive because managements had a good story to tell, and they had started telling it. Bank stocks did, in fact, have a good move in 1972, and I made about 50 percent on the bouquet of growth bank stocks I had bought for my hedge fund.

Then came the first oil shock of 1973, and the money center banks became involved in the recycling of petro-dollars. That is when the Euro-dollar market was born, and the great international lending boom began. Most of the business was conducted abroad, and United States banks formed holding companies to escape regulation at home. Many new financial instruments and financing techniques were invented, and banking became a much more sophisticated business than it had been only a few years earlier. There was a veritable explosion of international credit between 1973 and 1979. It was the foundation of the worldwide inflationary boom of the 1970s. The United States did not participate in the boom. It suffered from stagflation—a combination of rising inflation and high unemployment.

In 1979 a second oil shock reinforced the inflationary pressures. In order to bring inflation under control, the Federal Reserve adopted the monetarist doctrine propounded by Milton Friedman. Instead of controlling short-term interest rates, as it had done hitherto, the Federal Reserve fixed targets for money supply and allowed the rate on federal funds to fluctuate freely. The Federal Reserve's new policy was introduced in October 1979, and interest rates were already at record levels when President Ronald Reagan took office.

President Reagan believed in supply-side economics and a strong military posture. In his first budget, he cut taxes and increased military spending simultaneously. Although a concerted effort was made to reduce domestic spending, the savings were not large enough to offset the other two items. The path of least resistance led to a large budget deficit.

Since the budget deficit had to be financed within the limits of strict money supply targets, interest rates rose to unprecedented heights. Instead of economic expansion, the conflict between fiscal and monetary policy brought on a severe recession. Unexpectedly high interest rates, combined with a recession in the United States, prompted Mexico to threaten defaulting on its international debt obligations in August 1982. That was the inception of the international banking crisis of the 1980s, which devastated Latin America and other developing economies.

The Federal Reserve responded to the crisis by relaxing its grip on the money supply. The budget deficit was just beginning to accelerate. With the brakes released, the economy took off, and the recovery was as vigorous as the recession had been severe. It was aided by a spending spree by both the household and the corporate sectors, and it was abetted by the banking system. Military spending was just gearing up; the household sector enjoyed rising real incomes; the corporate sector benefited from accelerated depreciation and other tax concessions. Banks were eager to lend because practically any new lending had the effect of improving the quality of their loan portfolios. The demand emanating from all these sources was so strong that interest rates, after an initial decline, stabilized at historically high levels and eventually began to rise again. Foreign capital was attracted, partly by the high return on financial assets and partly by the confidence inspired by President Reagan. The dollar strengthened, and a strengthening currency combined with a positive interest rate differential made the move into the dollar irresistible. The strong dollar attracted imports, which helped to satisfy excess demand and to keep down the price level. A self-reinforcing process was set into motion in which a strong economy, a strong currency, a large budget deficit, and a large trade deficit mutually reinforced each other to produce noninflationary growth. In *The Alchemy of Finance* I called this circular relationship Reagan's Imperial Circle because it financed a strong military posture by attracting both goods and capital from abroad. This made the circle benign at the center and vicious at the periphery.* This was the beginning of the United States' current account deficit and the emergence of the United States as consumer of last resort that continued, with many gyrations, to the present day.

The international banking crisis was contained by the active and imaginative intervention of the authorities. Providing liquidity to the banking system was not enough. The amounts owed by sovereign borrowers far exceeded the

---

*I used Reagan's Imperial Circle as an example of a circular reflexive process as distinct from the boom-bust model.

banks' own capital; if the countries in question had been allowed to go into default, the banking system would have become insolvent. The last time that happened was in 1932, and it caused the Great Depression. Because of that experience such an outcome was unacceptable. Accordingly, the central banks exceeded their traditional role and banded together to bail out the debtor countries. A precedent of sorts had been established in England in 1974, when the Bank of England decided to bail out the so-called fringe banks that were outside its sphere of responsibility rather than to allow the clearing banks, from whom the fringe banks had borrowed heavily, to come under suspicion.* But the crisis of 1982 was the first time that the strategy of bailing out the debtors was applied on an international scale.

The central banks did not have sufficient authority to execute such a strategy, and makeshift arrangements had to be made in which the governments of all the creditor countries participated and the International Monetary Fund (IMF) played a key role. Rescue packages were put together for one country after another. Typically, commercial banks extended their commitments, the international monetary institutions injected new cash, and the debtor countries agreed to austerity programs designed to improve their balance of payments. In most cases, the commercial banks also had to come up with additional cash, enabling the debtor countries to stay current on their interest payments. The rescue packages constituted a remarkable achievement in international cooperation. The participants included the IMF, the Bank of International Settlements, a number of governments and central banks, and a

*This was, in turn, a precedent for the bailout of Bear Stearns in March 2008.

much larger number of commercial banks. In the case of Mexico, for instance, there were more than five hundred commercial banks involved.

I became a close student of the crisis and its resolution because I was fascinated by the systemic issues involved. I wrote a series of reports, distributed by Morgan Stanley, in which I analyzed the makeshift solution developed by the international financial authorities. I called it the Collective System of Lending. The Collective was held together by the fear of insolvency. Accordingly the integrity of the debt had to be preserved at all costs. That left the debtor countries to fend for themselves; they were granted some concessions on the terms of debt service, but each concession added to their future obligations. The debtor countries accepted this treatment in order to maintain access to capital markets and to avoid seizure of assets and because of fear of the unknown. The austerity programs did improve their trade balances, but in some cases the improvement could not keep pace with the accumulation of debt. Recognizing the problem, banks were building bad debt reserves; but at the time I reviewed the situation in *The Alchemy of Finance*, no way had been found to pass these reserves on to the debtor countries without destroying the principle that held the Collective together. Eventually the problem was solved by the introduction of Brady bonds, but most of Latin America lost a decade of growth.

On previous occasions credit crises led to stricter regulations of the offending entities in order to prevent a recurrence. But under the influence of market fundamentalism, which became the dominant creed in the Reagan years, the international banking crisis led to the opposite outcome:

Banks in the United States were granted greater freedom to make money. Practically all the restrictions that had been imposed on them in the Great Depression were gradually removed. They were allowed to expand their branches, merge across state lines, and enter new lines of business. The separation of investment banking and commercial banking faded until it disappeared altogether. Having been penalized by the Collective System of Lending, banks were anxious to avoid holding loans on their balance sheets; they preferred to package them and sell them off to investors who were not subject to supervision and persuasion by the regulatory authorities. Ever more sophisticated financial instruments were invented, and new ways to keep assets off balance sheets were found. That was when the super-bubble really took off.

The newly invented financial instruments and the newly introduced trading and financing techniques suffered from a fatal flaw. They were based on the assumption that financial markets tend towards equilibrium: They may temporarily deviate from it, but the deviations take the form of a random walk; eventually values revert to the established mean. Accordingly past experience was supposed to provide a reliable guide to the future. This assumption left out of account the impact of the new instruments and new techniques which changed the functioning of financial markets out of all recognition. I could vouch for that from personal experience: When I returned to the markets in the early 1990s after a few years' absence, I could not find my way around.

I date the inception of both globalization and the super-bubble to 1980, when Ronald Reagan and Margaret Thatcher came to power. The period since then was punctuated by occasional breakdowns in particular market segments. The international lending spree of the 1970s turned into the international banking crisis in 1982. The excessive use of portfolio insurance turned a stock market downdraft into an unprecedentedly steep drop in October 1987. Portfolio insurance involved the use of knock-out options. Because they were used on a large scale they could not be exercised without causing a catastrophic discontinuity. Similar episodes occurred on a smaller scale in other markets; I witnessed one in the dollar-yen exchange rate. The slicing up of mortgages into tranches caused a mini crash in the "toxic waste" tranche in 1994, which claimed a few victims. The Russian default in the emerging market crisis of 1998 led to the insolvency of Long-Term Capital Management (LTCM), a very large hedge fund using very high leverage, which threatened the stability of the financial system. It prompted the Fed to lower interest rates and arrange a cooperative rescue of LTCM by its lenders. These incidents did not lead to any regulatory reforms; on the contrary, the ability of the system to withstand these stresses reaffirmed the prevailing market fundamentalist creed and led to further relaxation of the regulatory environment.

Then came the technology bubble that burst in 2000 and the terrorist attack of September 11, 2001. To prevent a recession, the Fed lowered the federal funds rate to 1 percent and kept it there until June 2004. That engendered the housing bubble, in which financial innovations played a major role. With the spreading of risks, more risks could be taken. Unfortunately, the risks were passed on from those who were supposed to know them to others who were less familiar with them. What is worse, the newly invented methods and instruments were so sophisticated that the regulatory authorities lost the ability to calculate the risks involved. They came to depend on the risk control methods developed by the institutions themselves. The latest international agreement on the capital adequacy requirements of banks—Basel 2—allows the largest banks to rely on their own risk management systems. Something similar happened to the rating agencies who were supposed to evaluate the creditworthiness of the financial instruments. They came to rely on the calculations provided by the issuers of those instruments.

I find this the most shocking abdication of responsibility on the part of the regulators. If they could not calculate the risk, they should not have allowed the institutions under their supervision to undertake them. The risk models of the banks were based on the assumption that the system itself is stable. But, contrary to market fundamentalist beliefs, the stability of financial markets is not assured; it has to be actively maintained by the authorities. By relying on the risk calculations of the market participants, the regulators pulled up the anchor and unleashed a period of uncontrolled credit expansion. Specifically, value-at-risk (VAR) calculations are based on past experience. With unchecked credit expansions, the past became a poor guide to current conditions. VAR calculations allowed for two or three standard deviations. Higher standard deviations, which ought to have been extremely scarce, occurred with greater frequency. This ought to have been a warning signal, but it was largely ignored by regulators and participants alike. All they did was to introduce stress tests to measure how well they were prepared for the unexpected.

Similarly, the various synthetic mortgage securities were based on the assumption that the value of houses in the

United States taken as a whole never declines; individual regions may fluctuate, but the market as a whole is stable. That is what made securities spreading the risk over various regions seem more secure than individual mortgages. That assumption ignored the possibility of a nationwide housing bubble of the magnitude that actually occurred.

The regulatory authorities ought to have known better. After all, they had to intervene from time to time, and they knew that their intervention engendered a moral hazard. They paid lip service to the moral hazard, but when the chips were down they came to the rescue of institutions that were too big to fail. They knew that their intervention introduced asymmetric incentives that favored ever-increasing credit expansion, yet they were so carried away by the prevailing market fundamentalist mood and their own success that they came to believe that markets can self-regulate. That is how credit expansion came to reach unsustainable levels.

The right time to constrain credit expansion is during the expansionary phase. Central banks do respond to price and wage inflation but do not feel called upon to prevent asset price inflation.* Alan Greenspan did inveigh against the "irrational exuberance" of the stock market in December 1996 but did not go beyond words and stopped talking about it when his words did not have the desired affect. Greenspan had a more profound understanding of the economic processes than most experts, and he knew how to use the manipulative function in expressing his views. I was impressed by his forward-looking, dynamic approach, which stood in sharp

---

*The Federal Reserve focuses on so-called core prices, excluding energy and food.

contrast to the static, rearview-mirror assessment of European central bankers. He can be faulted, however, for allowing his Ayn Rand–inspired political views to intrude into his conduct as chairman of the Federal Reserve more than would have been appropriate. He supported the Bush tax cuts for the top 1 percent of the population and argued that the budget deficit should be reduced by cutting social services and discretionary spending. And keeping federal funds at 1 percent longer than necessary could have had something to do with the 2004 elections. Responsibility for the real estate bubble can be justly laid at his feet.

Ben Bernanke is more of a theoretician and does not have Greenspan's manipulative skills. He and the Bank of England's Mervyn King were acutely concerned with the moral hazard, and this had much to do with their belated response to the bursting of the housing bubble in 2007. The authorities consistently ignored or underestimated the abuses and excesses in the mortgage industry and their effect on the real economy. That is how the Federal Reserve fell so far behind the curve. The Federal Reserve had the legal authority to regulate the mortgage industry, which it failed to exercise. The Treasury also remained totally passive during this period and became active only when the crisis was well advanced. It introduced new regulations for the mortgage industry only after the industry ground to a standstill, and it confined itself to encouraging voluntary cooperation among lenders to mitigate the damage. That approach had worked in the international banking crisis of the 1980s because central banks could wield direct influence over the commercial banks involved. But the current crisis is incomparably more complicated because the mortgages have been sliced up, repackaged, and resold, and voluntary cooperation among unknown participants is difficult if not impossible to arrange. The attempt to create a so-called super-SIV (structured investment vehicle) to forestall the threat that SIVs would have to dump their assets was stillborn; and arrangements to provide relief to people who face a sudden jump in interest payments as their teaser rates expire in the next eighteen months will have only very limited effect. Mortgage service companies are overwhelmed and have no financial incentive to arrange for voluntary adjustments. There are some 2.3 million people in that category, many of whom have been duped by unscrupulous lenders. Altogether, the housing crisis will have far-reaching social consequences. One cannot expect this administration to do much about it. It will fall to the next administration to deal with a dismal reality. By that time it will be clearer exactly how dismal it is.

I was watching the evolution of the housing bubble from afar because I was not actively engaged in managing my funds. After my partner who ran the fund left in 2001, I converted my hedge fund into a less aggressively managed vehicle and renamed it an "endowment fund" whose primary task was to manage the assets of my foundations. Most of the money was farmed out to outside managers. Nevertheless, I could clearly see that a super-bubble was developing, and it was bound to end badly. I was on record predicting it in a book published in 2006. And I was not alone. The investment community was sharply divided between old fogeys like me and a younger generation who knew how to use the new instruments and techniques and believed in them. Of course, there were exceptions among them. One of them stood out: John Paulson, who bought insurance against the default of subprime mortgages, which returned a manifold profit on the premium he paid. I invited him to lunch to find out how he did it.

When the crisis erupted in August 2007, I considered the situation grave enough that I did not feel comfortable leaving the management of my fortune to others. I resumed control by establishing a "macro" trading account that gave the fund an overall posture overriding the positions managed by others. I believed that the developed world, particularly the United States, was heading for serious trouble, but there were powerful positive forces at work in other parts of the world, notably China, India, and some of the oil- and raw material–producing countries. We had built up substantial investment positions in the stock markets of those countries. I wanted to protect these positions by establishing substantial short positions in the developed world. I could use only blunt instruments like tradable stock indexes and currencies because I lacked detailed knowledge. Even so, the strategy was reasonably successful. It was not without ups and downs. The market became extremely volatile, and it took a lot of nerve to hold on to the short positions.

CHAPTER 7

My Outlook for 2008

In *The Alchemy of Finance* I conducted a real-time experiment where I documented my decision making as a hedge fund manager at the same time as I was making those decisions. I will repeat the exercise here.

JANUARY 1, 2008

The theory of reflexivity does not offer any firm predictions. It does help, however, to formulate some conjectures on what the future may hold in store.

1. A sixty-year period of credit expansion based on the United States exploiting its position at the center of the global financial system and its control over the international reserve currency has come to an end. The current financial crisis will have more severe and longer-lasting consequences than similar crises in the past. Every crisis involves a temporary credit contraction. The central banks will be able to pro-

vide temporary liquidity, as they did in the past, so that the acute phase of the crisis will be contained as usual; the international banking system will not break down as it did in the 1930s. But on previous occasions each crisis was followed by a new period of economic growth stimulated by easy money and new forms of credit growth. This time it will take much longer for growth to resume. The ability of the Federal Reserve to lower interest rates will be constrained by the unwillingness of the rest of the world to hold dollars and long-term dollar obligations. Some recently introduced financial instruments will have proven unsound and will go out of use. Some major financial institutions may yet prove insolvent, and credit will be harder to get. The extent of credit available for a given collateral will definitely shrink, and its cost will rise. The desire to borrow and take risk is also likely to abate. And one of the major sources of credit expansion, the United States' current account deficit, has definitely peaked. All this is bound to affect the U.S. economy negatively.

2. One can expect some longer-lasting changes in the character of banking and investment banking. These have been growth industries since 1972, launching ever more sophisticated new products and enjoying ever looser regulation. I expect this trend to be reversed. Regulators will try to regain control over the activities of the industry they are supposed to supervise. How far they will go will depend on the severity of the damage. If taxpayers' money is used, Congress will get involved. Finance constituted 14 percent of U.S. stock market capitalization at the end of the 1980s, 15 percent at the end of the 1990s, and peaked at 23 percent in

2006; I expect the percentage to be significantly lower ten years from now. On March 14, 2008, it was 18.2 percent.*

3. There are no grounds, however, for predicting a prolonged period of credit contraction or economic decline in the world as a whole because there are countervailing forces at work. China, India, and sbome oil-producing countries are experiencing dynamic developments which may not be significantly disrupted by the financial crisis and a recession in the United States. The United States recession itself will be cushioned by an improvement in the current account deficit.

4. The United States during the Bush administration failed to exercise proper political leadership. As a result the United States has suffered a precipitous decline in its power and influence in the world. The invasion of Iraq has much to do with the rise in the price of oil and the unwillingness of the rest of the world to hold dollars. A recession in the United States and the resilience of China, India, and the oil-producing countries will reinforce the decline in the power and influence of the United States. A significant part of the monetary reserves currently held in United States government bonds will be converted into real assets. This will reinforce and extend the current commodity boom and create inflationary pressures. The decline of the dollar as the generally accepted reserve currency will have far-reaching political consequences and raise the specter of a breakdown in the prevailing world order. Generally speaking, we are liable to

*Factset Research Systems Inc (analytical database). Finance includes major banks, regional banks, savings banks, finance leasing, investment banks, investment managers, financial conglomerates, insurance companies, and real estate investment trusts.

pass through a period of great uncertainty and destruction of financial wealth before a new order emerges.

These insights are too general to be of much use in practical decision making, but the theory itself, combined with known facts, does not carry us any further. Indeed, I was pushing the limits to get this far. To be more specific one needs to engage in guesswork.

As we enter the new year I find financial markets too pre-occupied with the liquidity crisis and not sufficiently aware of the long-term consequences. The central banks know how to provide liquidity and will do so, whatever it takes. They have already provided larger amounts against a wider range of collateral than ever before. So the acute phase of the crisis is bound to abate, but the fallout is yet to come. Both investors and the general public suffer from a misconception. They believe that the financial authorities—the Federal Reserve and the administration—will do whatever it takes to avoid a recession. I believe that they are not in a position to do so partly because of the commodity boom and partly because of the vulnerability of the dollar (the two are mutually self-rein-forcing). The world's willingness to hold dollars has been shaken. There are already too many dollars sloshing around, and the holders are eager to diversify. The major alternative reserve currency, the euro, has already been bid up to unsus-tainable levels, yet it is still under upward pressure. The fact that the Chinese renminbi has appreciated less than the euro has created tremendous trade frictions between China and Europe, and something has to give. I believe the renminbi will be allowed to appreciate at a faster rate. The forward premium on the renminbi is already over 8 percent per annum, and I believe the actual appreciation will be higher, although I cannot tell by how much. The Chinese authorities are hard to read, but there are a number of reasons why they should move in that direction. Most important is the threat of protectionism in the United States and now in Europe. An appreciating currency helps to moderate the irritation caused by a large trade surplus. It also helps moderate price inflation, which has become a problem for China. Since the inflation is driven mainly by the cost of imported fuel and food, currency appreciation is a direct antidote. In the past, there was resistance to a higher renminbi from the agricultural sector; with the rise in food prices, that consideration will carry less weight. All this is to the good. But a rising renminbi creates problems which are not properly understood.

The problem for China is that the real cost of capital is already negative, and faster currency appreciation pushes it further into negative territory. This creates an asset bubble. The process is already underway. Real estate is booming, and the Shanghai stock market index appreciated by 97 percent in 2007 and altogether by 420 percent since July 2005* when a four-year bear market ended. For reasons I shall explain in greater detail later, the bubble is still in an early stage, but it may be difficult to avoid a financial crisis later.

The problem for the United States is that a rising renminbi will cause prices at Wal-Mart to rise. A little inflation in a recessionary environment might be a good thing, but the Federal Reserve has to be concerned about the stability of the currency. I believe the Fed will continue to lower interest

*420 percent is the percentage change from the low close on July 11, 2005, to end 2007.

rates at a measured pace—1/4 percent every Open Market Committee meeting, probably without interruption—but a point will come when long-term interest rates will rise in response instead of falling. At that point the Fed will have reached the limits of its ability to stimulate the economy. Again, I do not know when this point will be reached, but I suspect it will be sooner rather than later.

There is much uncertainty about the prospect for a recession. Most economic forecasts still rate the chances at less than 50 percent. I cannot understand that. Housing prices will have to fall at least 20 percent over the next five years to get back to a normal relationship to household income. My boom-bust theory tells me that prices have to temporarily fall below the normal relationship in order to clear the market. This means that prices would have to fall by more than 20 percent within a year or so, or the market will not clear for years. At present the market is not clearing, as the latest statistics show. A decline of such magnitude is bound to affect consumer spending, employment, and overall business activity. The only countervailing force is the strength in exports, but that is bound to abate as the rest of the world slows down. Consumer spending has been remarkably resilient, and expectations are definitely erring on the positive side, with 65 percent of house owners expecting the value of their houses to moderately appreciate. My boom-bust theory tells me that participants will have to err on the negative side before the economy can turn positive. Whether we are in a recession now is questionable; that we shall slip into recession in the course of 2008 I consider a certainty.

The unraveling of the financial institutions has not yet run its course either. Year-end results are bound to contain some unpleasant surprises, and a recession is bound to cause further deterioration. There may be some additional shoes to drop. Collateralized debt obligations based on commercial real estate, particularly shopping malls, could easily unravel. Banks sold credit default swaps against their balance sheets, and as the recession progresses there may be some defaults. Markets will not be fully reassured until all the hidden liabilities are fully disclosed. The major investment banks have been very diligent in replenishing their balance sheets by raising capital, mainly from sovereign wealth funds, which hold out the promise of becoming the banking industry's salvation, but their appetite may soon become satiated. This may be yet another case where risks are transferred to those who understand them less well, and the prices paid by the first investors may prove to have been too high.

Europe is liable to be affected almost as badly as the United States. Spain, with its own real estate bubble, and the United Kingdom, given the importance of London as a financial center, are particularly vulnerable. European banks and pension funds are even more heavily weighed down with assets of doubtful value than American banks, and the overvaluation of the euro and sterling is going to hurt European economies. The Japanese economy is also doing poorly. The developed countries, taken together, make up 70 percent of the world economy. Nevertheless, I question whether the global economy will go into recession because of the very favorable dynamics that prevail in the oil-rich countries and some of the developing economies. Conventional wisdom says that when the United States sneezes the rest of the world catches cold. That used to be true, but no longer.

China is undergoing a radical structural transformation, and the asset bubble engendered by negative real interest rates is facilitating the process. State-owned enterprises are being transferred into private hands, and managements usually end up with significant stakes. Skillful managers used to make money on the side; now they find it advantageous to make money for the companies they manage and, to an increasing extent, own. Stocks listed on the Shanghai Stock Exchange may appear overvalued by conventional yardsticks (over forty times next year's earnings), but appearances may be deceptive when the motivation of management changes. No doubt a bubble is in formation, but it is in a relatively early stage, and there are powerful interests at work to keep the bubble going. The economic elite are eager to convert the perks of office they currently enjoy into ownership of property that they can pass on to their heirs. There is a long queue of companies whose managers are eager to get rid of state ownership, and they do not want to see the process interrupted. Nothing is quite as profitable as investing in an early-stage bubble.

I visited China in October 2005, and although I was no longer actively making investments, I saw greater opportunities there than at any time in my career. The Chinese economy had been growing at better than 10 percent a year over the past decade, but corporate earnings were not keeping pace with growth, and, after the initial euphoria that is characteristic of newly established stock markets, stocks had been in a bear market for the preceding four years. The government had just announced a scheme whereby all state-owned shares would become tradable within twenty-four months. I saw the opportunity of a lifetime, but I was not willing to go back into active money management, and I could not find a suitable Chinese partner. We did put some money to work in China, but, as always in these cases, not enough. The Shanghai index has risen by more than 400 percent since then.

China is exerting considerable influence on other emerging economies. It has shown an insatiable appetite for raw materials, and it has been the main motor of the boom in commodities and dry cargo shipping. In spite of the expected slowdown in the world economy, the price for iron ore is expected to rise at least 30 percent next year, with China as the largest customer. China has embarked on a shopping spree for mining, oil, and other raw material–producing companies. It is also ready to extend long-term credit on concessionary rates to African countries. It has come to rival the West as the source of capital inflows into Africa. China has also become the major trading partner of many Asian countries. (It is also becoming the largest producer of greenhouse gases in the world, but that is not the topic of discussion here.)

Undoubtedly, the recession in the developed world will adversely affect Chinese exports, but the domestic economy, and investments in and exports to the developing world, could take up much of the slack. The rate of growth will slow down, but the bubble, fueled by negative real interest rates, will continue to grow. The stock market index will certainly not continue to rise at the rate at which it did last year. Indeed, it may not rise at all, but the volume of new issues and the total size of the market will continue to grow unabated. The structural transformation of the economy will become more pronounced. Loss-making state-owned enterprises will more or less disappear, and what I call super state-owned enterprises—spin-offs from state-owned enterprises which are well managed and justify their high stock prices by absorbing additional assets from their mother company—will become a dominant feature of the market. The process will be somewhat similar to what I described as merger mania in the chapter "The 'Oligopolarization' of America" in *The Alchemy of Finance*, but much more dramatic. It may or may not come to a bad end, but in any case the end is several years away. In my judgment, China will sail through the current financial crisis and subsequent recession with flying colors and gain considerable relative strength.

The longer-term outlook for China is highly uncertain. It would not be surprising if the currently developing bubble ended in a financial crisis several years down the road. I said long ago that communism in China is likely to be brought to an end by a capitalist crisis. Alternatively, the transformation of China into a capitalist economy may be accomplished without a financial crisis. Either way, China is likely to challenge the supremacy of the United States much sooner than could have been expected when George W. Bush was elected president. What an ironic outcome for the Project for a New American Century! How to accommodate a surging China within the world order will be one of the most challenging tasks for the incoming administration.

I visited India at Christmastime in 2006, and I was even more positively impressed from an investment point of view than with China because India is a democracy with the rule of law. Moreover, it was technically easier to invest in India than in China. Market averages have more than doubled since that time. India used to grow at 3.5 percent per annum, barely higher than the population growth. The growth rate has now more than doubled. The groundwork of economic reforms was laid by the present prime minister, Manmohan Singh, when he was finance minister more than a decade ago, and it took some time for the dynamics of the economy to change. Information technology outsourcing served as the catalyst. Its growth was phenomenal. Last year India accounted for more than half the new jobs in that industry worldwide, but even today it represents less than 1 percent of total employment in India. The industry has passed its peak of profitability. There is a shortage of qualified labor, and profit margins are hurt by the appreciation of the currency. But the dynamics have spread to the rest of the economy.

The most spectacular has been the rise of the Ambani brothers. When their father, the founder of Reliance Industries, died, the brothers divided his empire among them and are now trying to outdo each other. Their activities range from oil refining, petrochemicals, and offshore natural gas production, to financial services and cellular telephones. The discovery of offshore natural gas promises to make India energy self-sufficient within the next few years. Mukesh Ambani is using the cash flow from its oil and gas business to set up Reliance Retail, bringing food directly from the grower to the consumer—a bold project that seeks to cut the differential between consumer and producer prices by more than half.

India's infrastructure lags far behind China's, but infrastructure investment is beginning to pick up, helped by domestic savings and capital inflows from the oil-rich Gulf States, which have large expatriate Indian populations. In these circumstances, I expect the Indian economy to perform well, although, after its stellar performance, the stock market may be vulnerable to correction.

Another source of strength for the world economy is to be found in some of the oil-producing countries of the Middle East (I don't discuss Russia because I don't want to invest there). These states are accumulating reserves at an impressive rate, by $122 billion in 2006 and by an estimated $114 billion in 2007, to a reserve level of $545 billion.* They are eager to diversify out of dollar denominated bonds and have all set up sovereign wealth funds whose assets are growing rapidly. The Gulf States have decided to invest in developing their own economies by exploiting their access to cheap energy, building oil refining and petrochemical plants, aluminum smelters, and other heavy industries at a rate which is limited only by the shortage of labor and equipment. Due to their competitive advantage, they are likely to become dominant factors in these industries. Abu Dhabi has decided to establish a metropolis to rival Dubai. With over a trillion dollars in reserves and a population of 1.6 million (80 percent are expatriates), they can afford to do so. The forced pace of development has created inflationary pressures and there is a strong case for unpegging the currencies from the dollar. Kuwait has already done so, but the other states, particularly Saudi Arabia, have been dissuaded from following Kuwait's example by strong political pressure from Washington. The dollar pegs, coupled with domestic inflation, have brought about negative real interest rates. The stock markets of the Gulf States are emerging from a severe crash that followed

*International Monetary Fund World Economic and Financial Surveys, October 2007. The countries behind these numbers include: Bahrain, Iran, Iraq, Kuwait, Libya, Oman, Qatar, Saudi Arabia, and the United Arab Emirates. Saudi Arabia's gross reserves include investments in foreign securities, which are excluded in the reporting of official reserves.

the initial euphoria, and negative real interest rates are attracting capital inflows from abroad, just as in China. That is
the perverse effect of dollar pegs, although in the case of the
Gulf States—with the exception of Kuwait—the peg is not
crawling. I believe the dynamics are strong enough—despite
the political risks posed by Iran—to withstand a worldwide
slowdown. Any lowering of interest rates in the United
States would increase the pressure to break the peg.

Sovereign wealth funds are becoming important players in
the international financial system. Their current size is estimated at about $2.5 trillion, and they are growing rapidly.
They have already invested $28.65 billion in ailing financial
institutions.* China has allocated $5 billion to investing in
Africa. Sovereign wealth funds are likely to emerge as lenders
and investors of last resort similar to the role that Japan sought
to play after the stock market crash of 1987. But the sovereign
wealth funds are more diverse than the Japanese financial institutions were, and they are likely to follow divergent paths.
The financial crisis is likely to make them more welcome in
the West than they would have been otherwise. It will be re-
called that a Chinese state-owned oil company, China National Offshore Oil Corporation, ran into political opposition
when it tried to acquire Unocal, as did a Dubai company, DP
World, when it sought to take control of American port facilities. To the extent that one can generalize, sovereign wealth
funds are likely to favor investing in the developing world,

---

*July 13, 2007, Temasek Holdings, $2.0 billion in Barclays PLC; November 26,
2007, Abu Dhabi Investment Authority, $7.5 billion in Citigroup Inc.; Decem-
ber 10, 2007, Government of Singapore Investment Corp., $9.75 billion in UBS
AG; December 19, 2007, China Investment Corp. $5.0 billion in Morgan Stanley;
December 24, 2007, Temasek Holdings, at least $4.4 billion in Merrill Lynch.

limited only by the absorptive capacity of those countries. That is likely to reinforce the positive performance of the developing economies. Sovereign wealth funds are also likely to become significant stakeholders in the United States economy unless prevented by protectionist measures.

Whether the global slowdown will turn into a global recession is an open question. One can, however, predict with a fair degree of certainty that the developing world will perform much better than the developed countries. This may set up an eventual reversal, when the investments in raw material production will have created overcapacity.

In 2007, being long in emerging markets and short in the stock markets of the developed world was a rewarding investment strategy. I expect that this will continue to be the case in 2008 but with a significant shift of emphasis from being net long to being net short. Due to the change in character of my fund from a pure hedge fund to an endowment fund, and my reduced role in managing it, I do not consider it appropriate to give a detailed account of our investment positions as I did in the real-time experiment published in *The Alchemy of Finance*. I can, however, summarize my investment strategy for 2008 in one sentence: short U.S. and European stocks, U.S. ten-year government bonds, and the U.S. dollar; long Chinese, Indian, and Gulf States stocks and non-U.S. currencies.

JANUARY 6, 2008

The real-time experiment is off to a better start than I expected. We are making money both with our longs and shorts, and currencies. Only our short position in ten-year

U.S. government bonds is working against us, but this was to be expected; bonds and stocks tend to move in opposite directions. I took on the position knowing that I may be early, but with a depreciating dollar I believe it will eventually prove to be right, and in the meantime it reduces the volatility of the portfolio. In keeping with our character of an endowment fund rather than a regular hedge fund, our exposure is relatively modest: less than half our equity in any one direction. Nevertheless, the fund is up more than 3 percent in three trading days.

I started thinking about when to cover my short positions. Certainly not yet. The market has just started to recognize that a recession is in store; it has to fall below the lows of 2007. For the next six months the surprises are likely to be on the negative side. I do not expect this administration to be capable of producing any policy measures that would meaningfully improve the situation. The market may, of course, establish a tradable bottom sooner than six months—I am not very good at picking bottoms.

MARCH 10, 2008

I got the big picture right in my predictions for 2008, but there were some minor deviations which have had a major impact both on the course of events and on our investment performance.

- The disruption of the financial system has been worse than I expected. Markets that I did not even know existed—such as the auction-rated municipal bond market—fell apart.

Credit spreads continued to widen, and losses continued to mount. Banks and brokers have recently raised their margin requirements, and leveraged hedge funds are forced to deleverage. Some are being liquidated. There are still some shoes left to drop; the gigantic credit default swap market has yet to unravel. Write-offs are likely to peak in the first quarter of 2008. There may be further losses in later quarters, but not at the same rate.

- Commodity markets stayed stronger than I expected. The rise in iron ore prices was 60 percent, not 30 percent. Gold is approaching $1,000 an ounce.

- The Federal Reserve swung around more violently than I expected. It dropped the federal funds rate by an unprecedented three-quarter percent in an emergency meeting on January 22 and moved another half percent at its regular meeting on January 30.

- In spite of its dramatic turnaround, the Fed was unable to bring down mortgage rates, but for a different reason than the one I anticipated. It was the widening of credit spreads, not the steepening of the yield curve, that pushed up mortgage rates. The yield on ten-year government bonds dropped sharply, and our short position turned out to be very costly.

- The Indian market had a big fall. We had failed to cut back on our long positions and took it on the chin. Losses in these two positions (China has not hurt us much) offset most of our gains in the macro-account. As a result we are barely ahead for the year.

Having increased our short positions in the dollar and in U.S. and European stock indexes and financial stocks, and slightly reduced our government bond shorts, we seem to be well positioned for the period immediately ahead. I expect a re-test of the January stock market bottom with financial stocks making new lows but the market as a whole holding above. This may lead to a tradable rally, but I foresee lower lows in the months ahead.

A new chief investment officer joined me recently; this will allow me to distance myself from the markets. We intend to cover some or most of our financial shorts in the re-test and maybe go long in some stocks that will benefit from a lower dollar and then establish new shorts on the rally. The new CIO knows the bond markets well. He is accumulating some of the higher-grade mortgage indexes and intends to increase our shorts in long-term government bonds in due course.

March 16, 2008

This has been a dramatic week. The deleveraging of hedge funds continued, and some are being forcibly liquidated, putting downward pressure on securities and upward pressure on credit spreads. The dollar is making new lows, with the euro breaking through $1.55 and the yen breaking 100 to the dollar. Pressures in the currency markets are intensifying. Both the Chinese and the Gulf currencies are straining against their dollar pegs. On Thursday, Bear Stearns came under suspicion as a counterparty, forcing the Fed to come to the rescue on Friday by opening the credit window to Bear through the intermediation of JP Morgan. The panic is palpable. We continued to add to the dollar shorts, but we started going against the decline in the stock market and the continued rise in government bonds. We also bought some Bear Stearns shares and sold some Bear Stearns credit default swaps on Friday (the first time we traded in that market) in the expectation that Bear Stearns will be auctioned off by the Fed over the weekend. This is a short-term, finite bet that either pays off on Monday or has to be taken off the table. The result to date is a standoff; the fund continues to tread water, with the macro-account making money and the rest of the fund losing. Our only consolation is that the portfolio is much less volatile than the markets. It would be better to show a profit.

MARCH 20, 2008

Another eventful week. Bear Stearns was not auctioned off but forced into the hands of JP Morgan at $2 a share. We were half right: made money on the credit default swaps but lost on the shares—a wash. The shareholders of Bear are squealing, but are probably powerless. We forgot to take into account that Bear is disliked by the establishment, and the Fed would use the occasion to deal with the moral hazard by punishing the shareholders.

The markets were shocked by the Fed's action, and we had some kind of a selling climax on Monday. We used the occasion to cover our remaining shorts in financial stocks, and we were almost neutral in our stock exposure by Tuesday morning, betting that Lehman Brothers, which came under siege on Monday, would be able to withstand the onslaught. We were right, and after the Fed cut rates by another 75 basis points stocks staged the best rally of the year. This ought to have been a tradable rally, lasting at least a few weeks, but the stock market broke all the rules and reversed itself on Wednesday. In every boom-bust sequence people come to believe that the normal rules do not apply, but they usually do. This time it really is different, confirming my thesis that this crisis is not like the other ones. To top it off, the dollar staged a sharp rally on Thursday morning, causing some damage to the macro-account. The fund is now under water for the year. I ascribe the dollar rally to the liquidation of speculative positions, some forced and some technical. I intend to hold my positions, but I am prepared to see further losses. One of the advantages of low leverage is that I can afford it.

I have to end the real-time experiment because the manuscript has to go to the publisher. I would have preferred to end it with a profit for the overall fund, not just the macro-account, but this result may be more appropriate for the purposes of this book. We are in a period of forced deleveraging and the destruction of financial wealth. It is difficult to escape it.

March 23, 2008

In writing the conclusion to my book I gained a new insight into what is to be expected for the rest of 2008. It will guide my investment decisions. I shall conclude the real-time experiment by quoting the key passage:

> Eventually, the U.S. government will have to use taxpayers' money to arrest the decline in house prices. Until it does, the decline will be self-reinforcing, with people

walking away from homes in which they have negative equity and more and more financial institutions becoming insolvent, thus reinforcing both the recession and flight from the dollar. The Bush administration and most economic forecasters do not understand that markets can be self-reinforcing on the downside as well as the upside. They are waiting for the housing market to find a bottom on its own, but it is further away than they think.

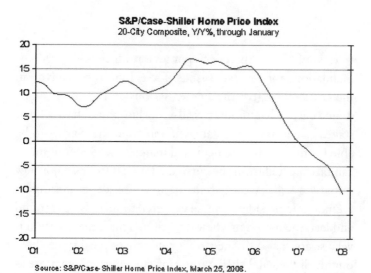

S&P/Case-Shiller Home Price Index
20-City Composite, Y/Y%, through January

Source: S&P/Case-Shiller Home Price Index, March 25, 2008.

CHAPTER 8

Some Policy Recommendations

It would be premature to put forward firm policy recommendations for several reasons. First, I am too involved in the markets to give the matter serious consideration. The drama currently unfolding is all-absorbing, and I have a lot at stake. I shall have to distance myself from the market to be able to think in a more detached manner. Second, not much can be expected from the current administration. Major new initiatives will have to await the new president, and only a Democratic president can be expected to turn things around and lead the nation in a new direction. Third, the situation is very serious, and the new policy initiatives need to be thoroughly discussed. I shall outline my current thinking more as subjects for discussion than as firm conclusions.

Clearly an unleashed and unhinged financial industry is wreaking havoc with the economy. It needs to be reined in. Credit creation by its nature is a reflexive process. It needs to be regulated in order to prevent excesses. We must remember, however, that regulators are not only human but also bureaucratic. Going overboard with regulations could severely impede economic activity. A return to the conditions that prevailed after World War II would be a big mistake. Credit availability fosters not only productivity but also flexibility and innovation. Credit creation should not be put into a straitjacket. The world is full of uncertainty, and markets can adjust to changing conditions much better than bureaucrats. At the same time, we must recognize that markets do not just passively adjust to changing circumstances but also actively contribute to shaping the course of events. They may create the instabilities and uncertainties that make their flexibility so valuable. This has to be taken into account in formulating macroeconomic policies. Markets should be given the greatest possible scope compatible with maintaining economic stability.

In large part the excesses in the financial markets are due to the regulators' failure to exercise proper control. Some of the newly introduced financial instruments and methods were based on false premises. They have shown themselves to be unsustainable, and therefore they will have to be abandoned. But others help to spread or hedge against risks and need to be preserved. The regulators need to gain a better understanding of the recent innovations, and they ought not to allow practices that they do not fully understand. The idea that risk management can be left to the participants was an aberration. There are systemic risks that need to be managed by the regulatory authorities. To be able to do so they must have adequate information. The participants, including hedge funds and sovereign wealth funds and other unregulated entities, must provide that information even if it is costly and cumbersome. The costs pale into insignificance when compared to the costs of a breakdown.

Moral hazard poses a thorny problem, but it can be resolved. Let's face it: When the financial system is endangered, the authorities must cave in. Whether they like it or not, institutions engaged in credit creation must accept the fact that they are being protected by the authorities. They must, therefore, pay a price for it. The authorities must exercise more vigilance and control during the expansionary phase. That will undoubtedly limit the profitability of the business. The people engaged in the business will not like it and will lobby against it, but credit creation has to be a regulated business. Regulators ought to be held accountable if they allow matters to get out of hand so that an institution has to be rescued. In recent years matters did get out of hand. The financial industry was allowed to get far too profitable and far too big.

The most important lesson to be learned from the current crisis is that the monetary authorities have to be concerned not only with controlling the money supply but also with credit creation. Monetarism is a false doctrine. Money and credit do not go hand in hand. Monetary authorities have to be concerned not only with wage inflation but also with avoiding asset bubbles. Asset prices depend not only on the availability of money but also on the willingness to lend. The monetary authorities have to monitor and take into account not only money supply but also credit conditions. It will be objected that asking the monetary authorities to control asset prices gives them one too many tasks to perform. The objection would be valid if the task of the monetary authorities could be confined to applying certain rules mechanically. Their job is more complicated than that. They are engaged in a delicate game of managing expectations using all the tricks involved in the exercise of the manipulative function. That is an art, and it cannot be reduced to science. Alan Greenspan was a grand master of the manipulative function. Unfortunately he put his skills at the service of the wrong cause; he was too much of a market fundamentalist.

Both the housing bubble and the super-bubble have been characterized by the excessive use of leverage. This was supported by sophisticated risk management models that calculated known risks but ignored the uncertainties inherent in reflexivity. If they do nothing else, regulators must reassert control over the use of leverage. They used to exercise such control. Equities are still subject to margin requirements, although these have become largely meaningless because there are so many ways around them. Mortgage securities and other synthetic instruments were never brought under control because they were introduced during the market fundamentalist era. Controlling leverage will reduce both the size and the profitability of the financial industry, but that is what the public interest demands.

One specific measure that could help relieve the credit crisis is the establishment of a clearing house or exchange for credit default swaps. Forty-five trillion dollars worth of contracts are outstanding and those who hold the contracts do not know whether their counterparties have adequately protected themselves. If and when defaults occur some of the counterparties are likely to prove unable to fulfill their obligations. This prospect overhangs the market like a Damocles Sword that is bound to fall, but not yet. It must have played a role in the Fed's decision not to allow Bear Sterns to fail. There is much to be gained by establishing a clearing house or exchange with a sound capital structure and strict margin requirements to which all existing and future contracts would have to be submitted.

What is to be done about the mess created by the bursting of the housing bubble? The usual anti-cyclical monetary and fiscal policies are appropriate as far as they go, but for the reasons I have given, they will not go far enough. Additional measures are needed to contain the collapse in house prices and alleviate the pain connected with it. For both these reasons it is desirable to let as many people keep their homes as possible. This applies both to the holders of subprime mortgages and to the people whose mortgages exceed the value of their houses. They may be considered victims of the housing bubble deserving some relief. But giving them relief is tricky because mortgages derive their value from the fact that they can be enforced by foreclosure. In most other countries borrowers are personally liable, while in the United States lenders usually have no recourse other than foreclosure. On the other hand, foreclosures depress house prices and aggravate the slump. They are also costly to all parties involved and result in negative spillover effects. What can be done to balance these considerations? This is a subject to which I have given more detailed consideration than the other issues I have discussed so far, and I have also involved my foundation, the Open Society Institute. Here are my preliminary findings.

About 40 percent of the 7 million subprime loans outstanding will default in the next two years. The defaults of option-adjustable-rate mortgages and other mortgages subject to rate reset will be of the same order of magnitude but over a somewhat longer period of time. This will maintain the downward pressure on house prices. Prices are likely to fall below the long-term trend unless arrested by government intervention.

The human suffering caused by the housing crisis will be enormous. There is significant evidence that senior citizens were targeted for some of the worst predatory practices and are disproportionately defaulting on their mortgages. Communities of color are also disproportionately affected. Given that home ownership is a key factor in increasing wealth and opportunity in the United States, upwardly mobile young professionals of color will be particularly hard hit. They bought into the promise of the "ownership society," and their assets are concentrated in home ownership. Prince George's County, Maryland, offers a prime example. It is one of the most prosperous predominantly black counties in the nation, yet it is experiencing the highest number of foreclosures in Maryland. Data for Maryland show that 54 percent of African American homeowners have subprime loans, compared to 47 percent for Hispanics and 18 percent for Whites.

Foreclosures reduce the value of surrounding houses, pushing additional home owners to abandon their property because their mortgages exceed the values of their houses. Ultimately, concentrated foreclosures destabilize entire neighborhoods and have repercussions in other areas, such as employment, education, health, and child well-being. Avoiding foreclosure ought to be the primary focus of additional policy measures. The already enacted initiatives of the Bush administration do not amount to more than exercises in public relations. Once you apply all the limitations you are left with practically nothing.

Both systemic and individualized approaches are needed. As regards the need for systemic intervention, I believe that

Representative Barney Frank is on the right track, although in order to gain bipartisan support he does not go far enough. He put forward two proposals that would strike the right balance between protecting the right to foreclosure and discouraging the exercise of that right—if they were adopted in the sequence that he proposes. First, he would modify the bankruptcy law so that a bankruptcy judge could rewrite mortgage loan terms on a principal residence. This would put pressure on the lenders to voluntarily modify such mortgages in order to avoid a compulsory modification of the mortgage, or a "cram down." The objection from the Republican side is that it would impinge on the rights of the lender and therefore make mortgages more expensive in the future. But the Frank proposal only applies to mortgages originated between January 2005 and June 2007. Moreover, the current bankruptcy law already allows modifications of mortgages on second homes, and it has not affected their cost appreciably.

Second, Frank would empower the Federal Housing Administration (FHA) to provide guarantees that would help refinance subprime borrowers into affordable mortgages. The holders of the original loan would be paid off from the proceeds of a new FHA-insured loan at no more than 85 percent of the current appraised value of the house. To compensate the FHA for providing guarantees, the FHA would retain a second lien on the property. When the borrower sells the home or refinances the loan, the borrower will pay from any profit of the higher of (1) an ongoing exit fee equal to 3 percent of the original FHA loan balance; or (2) a declining percentage of any profits (e.g., from 100 percent in year one to 20 percent in year five and 0 percent thereafter). After year five, only the 3 percent exit fee will apply.

Both the strength and the weakness of this proposal is that it is voluntary. On the positive side, it does not violate the right to foreclosure. On the negative side, it applies only to a rather narrow segment of troubled mortgages. It is confined to borrowers whose income is at least two-and-a-half times their debt service costs. At the same time, the mortgage holders must be willing to accept 85 percent of the current market value as payment in full without participating in any potential future upside in the home value. Frank's FHA proposal may well pass into law under the Bush administration but it is unlikely to have much impact on the housing crisis. It will have to be substantially enlarged before it makes a meaningful difference. The bankruptcy modification, by contrast, would be meaningful, but it is opposed by the Bush administration.

According to the mortgage industry, there are a number of legal and practical impediments that prevent loan servicers from modifying subprime loans facing delinquency and default. Servicers argue that securitization of mortgages makes it difficult to track individual loans and that "pooling and servicing agreements" substantially limit their discretion to alter loan terms. But the main impediment is "tranche warfare." Different tranches have competing interests in a given loan—one tranche may have a priority claim to the principal, another to the interest. Servicers resist rewriting mortgages because one tranche inevitably will take a deeper hit than others, and servicers are accountable to all tranches simultaneously.

There is a growing consensus, however, that pooling and servicing agreements allow greater flexibility than previously acknowledged. Notwithstanding the problems of securitizations, Moody's confirms that the rate of loan modifications is on the rise, but it still accounted for only 3.5 percent of the loans that reset in 2007. More attention should be devoted to quantifying and documenting the benefits of loan modifications in order to persuade lenders to put additional pressure on their servicers to engage in workouts.

Unfortunately, however, even with sweeping reforms, many homeowners will be unable to afford to stay in their homes. Local governments will need to come to terms with the fact that a significant share of homeowners will lose their homes. And because the most unscrupulous lending was concentrated in communities of color, which are the most vulnerable financially, local governments face the daunting prospect of huge inventories of distressed properties being dumped on the market in precisely those neighborhoods least equipped to absorb the shock. The trick here will be to ensure that those properties do not fall vacant or into the hands of absentee owners, but rather are quickly transferred to responsible buyers who occupy and maintain their homes.

Helping local communities will be a fertile field for private philanthropy. Matching funds from the federal and state governments could greatly increase its scope and impact. My foundation is sponsoring local initiatives in New York City and Maryland.

In New York City, we have initiated the Center for New York City Neighborhoods with funding from New York City government, private philanthropy, and the lending industry. It will increase and coordinate foreclosure prevention advocacy, including counseling and referral services, legal assistance, loan remediation, and preventive outreach and education. Its primary mission is to keep borrowers in their homes. For those who are unable to stay in their homes, it will support the efficient transfer of properties to responsible homeowners or nonprofit organizations to ensure neighborhood stability. We are hopeful that it will assist as many as eighteen thousand borrowers annually. The Center for New York City Neighborhoods will serve as an honest broker, facilitating communication among borrowers, direct service providers, and the lending industry. Although New York City's housing market has not been hardest hit by the current crisis, I hope that local solutions piloted in New York will serve as a model for other communities.

Various efforts are underway in Maryland to assist homeowners in or near default on their mortgages. The Baltimore Homeownership Preservation Coalition and a similar coalition in Prince George's County offer homeowners in trouble a place they can turn to which has their best interests at heart. The limiting factor is the lack of well-trained counselors. We plan to support various training schemes, some of which will likely receive state support.

We are studying what else can be done.

Conclusion

My main purpose in writing this book is to demonstrate the validity and importance of reflexivity. The moment is auspicious. Not only has the prevailing paradigm—equilibrium theory, and its political derivative, market fundamentalism—proven itself incapable of explaining the current state of affairs, it can be held responsible for landing us in the mess we are in. We badly need a new paradigm. But the new paradigm I am proposing—the recognition of reflexivity—still has to prove its worth. Until now it could not compete with equilibrium theory because it could not provide unequivocal predictions. That is why it was not given any serious consideration by economists. Now that equilibrium theory has shown itself to be such a failure at both prediction and explanation, the field is more open. The idea that reflexivity introduces an element of uncertainty into human affairs in general and financial markets in particular must be given some credence. But the theory must still show what it can do. I have done what I can by way of explanation. I have also used my conceptual framework to guide me in my investment decisions. Still, I believe I could do more in drawing on that framework as well as a lifetime of experience (the two are interconnected) to figure out what lies ahead. I claim that we are at the end of an era. What will the new era look like?

Firm predictions are out of the question. The future depends on the policy responses the financial crisis will provoke. But we can identify the problems and analyze the policy options. We can also make some firm predictions about what the next era will *not* look like. The post–World War II period of credit expansion will not be followed by an equally long period of credit contraction. Boom-bust processes are asymmetric in shape: a long, gradually accelerating boom is followed by a short and sharp bust. Consequently, most of the credit contraction can be expected to occur in the near term. House prices have already declined nearly 10 percent, and they are liable to decline another 20 percent or more in the next year. The deleveraging of hedge funds and bank balance sheets is also in full swing; it cannot continue at the current rate much longer. It may receive new impetus from a recession or other dislocations; nevertheless, it can be expected to run its course within a year or so. The end of the credit contraction is liable to bring some short-term relief, but it is unlikely to be followed by a resumption of credit expansion at anything like the rates to which we have become accustomed.

While a recession in the United States is now (April 2008) inevitable, there is no reason yet to expect a global recession. Powerful expansionary forces are at work in other parts of the world, and they may well counterbalance a recession in the United States and a slowdown in Europe and Japan. Economic developments may of course have political repercussions that could disrupt the world economy.

In the same vein, the end of the super-bubble does not mean the end of all bubbles. On the contrary, new bubbles are already in formation. The flight from the dollar has reinforced an already extended boom in raw materials and energy. Biofuel legislation has generated a boom in agricultural products. And the appreciation of the renminbi has caused real interest rates in China to turn negative, and that is usually associated with an asset bubble.

So what does the end of an era really mean? I contend that it means the end of a long period of relative stability based on the United States as the dominant power and the dollar as the main international reserve currency. I foresee a period of political and financial instability, hopefully to be followed by the emergence of a new world order.

To appreciate what is in store I have to explain one of the corollaries of my conceptual framework to which I have not given sufficient emphasis until now. I have spoken of the postulate of radical fallibility, the idea that all human constructs are flawed in one way or another, although the flaws may not become apparent until a construct has been in existence for a while. It follows that flawed constructs can be stable for extended periods. I have also spoken of a fundamental difference between natural and social science. One of the ways in which the difference manifests itself is that machines that utilize the forces of nature must obey the laws of nature; they must be what analytical philosophers call "well formed." Power stations must produce electricity, combustion engines must burn fuel in a controlled manner, nuclear weapons must release the energy contained in the nuclei of atoms in an explosion, and so on. Social arrangements need not deliver on their promises in the same way; it is enough if people can be persuaded to accept them for one reason or another, be it persuasion, tradition, or compulsion. Indeed, social arrangements can never be "well formed" because of the innate inability of participants to base their decisions purely on knowledge. Whatever regime prevails, it is liable to contain unresolved contradictions, and it may be succeeded by a totally different regime in short order.

What I am trying to explain in this abstract manner I have experienced in a very tangible form during my lifetime. I grew up in a stable, middle-class environment; then the Nazis would have killed me if my father had not arranged for me a false identity. I experienced the beginnings of Communist repression in Hungary; then I was an outsider in England, looking in on a stable, self-contained society. I saw the financial markets transformed out of all recognition in the course of fifty years, and I became somebody out of a nobody.

As I look at history, I see stable periods come and go. Now I see a relatively stable period going. I can identify enormous inconsistencies in the prevailing arrangements. They are not new; indeed they are inevitable in the sense that no arrangements are known that would avoid them. Take the exchange rate system. Every currency regime has its shortcomings. Fixed exchange rates are too rigid and prone to break down; floating exchange rates tend to swing too much; managed floats and crawling pegs tend to reinforce the trend they seek to moderate. I used to joke that currency regimes resemble matrimonial regimes: Whatever regime prevails, its opposite looks more attractive. Or consider the prevailing world order. There is something inconsistent about a globalized economy and political arrangements based on the principle of sovereignty. These inconsistencies were present in the era which is now coming to an end, but the dominance of the United States and the dollar introduced a sense of stability. Something has happened to disrupt that stability. The policies pursued by the Bush administration have impaired the political dominance of the United States, and now a financial crisis has endangered the international financial system and reduced the willingness of the rest of the world to hold dollars.

In my boom-bust model, far-from-equilibrium conditions are characteristic of the later stages of a bubble, to be followed by a return to more normal, near-equilibrium conditions. In this respect the super-bubble does not follow my boom-bust model, because there are no normal, near-equilibrium conditions to return to. We are facing a period of greatly increased uncertainty where the range of possible outcomes is much broader than in normal times. The greatest uncertainty revolves around the response of the U.S. authorities to the predicament that confronts them.

The United States is facing both a recession and a flight from the dollar. The decline in housing prices, the weight of accumulated household debt, and the losses and uncertainties in the banking system threaten to push the economy into a self-reinforcing decline. Measures to combat this threat increase the supply of dollars. At the same time, the flight from the dollar has set up inflationary pressures through higher energy, commodity, and food prices. The European Central Bank, whose mission is to maintain price stability, is reluctant to lower interest rates. This has created a discord between U.S. and E.U. monetary policy and put upward pressure on the euro. The euro has appreciated more than the renminbi, creating trade tension between Europe and China. The renminbi can be expected to catch up with the euro both to avoid protectionism in the United States and increasingly in Europe, and to contain imported price inflation in China. This will, in turn, increase prices at Wal-Mart and put additional pressure on the already beleaguered U.S. consumer. Unfortunately this administration shows no understanding of the predicament in which it finds itself.

Eventually, the U.S. government will have to use taxpayers' money to arrest the decline in house prices. Until it does, the decline will be self-reinforcing, with people walking away from homes in which they have negative equity and more and more financial institutions becoming insolvent, thus reinforcing both the recession and flight from the dollar. The Bush administration and most economic forecasters do not understand that markets can be self-reinforcing on the downside as well as the upside. They are waiting for the housing market to find a bottom on its own, but it is further away than they think. The Bush administration resists using taxpayers' money because of its market fundamentalist ideology and its reluctance to yield power to Congress. It has left the conduct of policy largely to the Federal Reserve. This has put too much of a burden on an institution designed to deal with liquidity, not solvency, problems. With the Bear Stearns rescue operation and the latest-term security lending facility, the Fed has put its own balance sheet at risk. I expect better of the next administration. Until then, I foresee many policy turns and changes in market direction since current policies are inadequate. It will be difficult to stay ahead of the curve.

*   *   *

I release this book at the present time with grave misgivings. I am afraid that there will be a conflict between my interest in writing the book and the interest of those who will read it, particularly in the electronic edition. Near panic conditions prevail in financial markets. People want to know what lies ahead. I cannot tell them because I do not know. What I want to tell them is something different. I want to explain the human condition.

We have to make decisions without having sufficient knowledge at our disposal. We have gained control over the forces of nature. That makes us very powerful. Our decisions have great impact. We can do a lot of good or a lot of harm. But we have not learned how to govern ourselves. As a consequence, we live in great uncertainty and grave danger. We need to gain a better understanding of the situation in which we find ourselves. It is difficult to accept uncertainty. It is tempting to try and escape it by kidding ourselves and each other, but that is liable to land us in greater difficulties.

My life has been devoted to gaining a better understanding of reality. In this book I have focused on the financial markets because they provide an excellent laboratory for testing my theories, and I have rushed into print because this is a moment when a prevailing misconception has landed us in grave difficulties. This should at least demonstrate how important it is to confront reality instead of trying to escape it. We can, of course, never fully comprehend reality, and I do not pretend that reflexivity constitutes the ultimate truth. The theory claims that the ultimate truth is beyond our human reach and explores the role that misconceptions play in shaping the course of events. That is not what people are interested in when financial markets are in turmoil. But I hope they will be willing to give it some consideration. In return, I hope I have given them some insight into what goes on in the financial markets.

I should like to end with a plea. Let this not be the conclusion but the beginning of a concerted effort at better understanding the human condition. Given our increased control over the forces of nature, how can we govern ourselves better? How is the new paradigm for financial markets to be reconciled with the old one? How should financial markets be regulated? How can the international financial system be reformed? How can we deal with global warming and nuclear proliferation? How can we bring about a better world order? These are the questions for which we have to find answers. I hope to participate in a lively debate.

Acknowledgments

Normally I would circulate my manuscript widely and keep revising it based on the comments I receive. On this occasion I did not have time to do that. Just a few people gave me valuable feedback: Keith Anderson, Jennifer Chun, Leon Cooperman, Martin Eakes, Charles Krusen, John Heimann, Marcel Kasumovich, Richard Katz, Bill McDonough, Pierre Mirabaud, Mark Notturno, Jonathan Soros, Paul Soros, Herb Sturz, Michael Vachon, and Byron Wien. I did receive invaluable assistance on the philosophical part from Colin McGinn, who commented on the text in detail and helped me over some conceptual difficulties. Charles Morris, whose book* I can heartily recommend, understands the intricacies of synthetic financial instruments much better than I do. He and Marcel Kasumovich helped me with the Introduction and Part 2. Raquiba LaBrie and Herb Sturz from my foundation organized a meeting of experts on the foreclosure problem. They along with Solomon Greene and Diana Morris helped with the policy recommendations relating to the subject. Keith Anderson supplied the charts I used in Chapter 5. My publisher, Peter Osnos, and the entire PublicAffairs team

*Charles R. Morris, *The Trillion Dollar Meltdown: Easy Money, High Rollers, and the Great Credit Crash* (New York: PublicAffairs, 2008).

achieved the impossible by publishing the book electronically within a few days of my submitting the final text. Yvonne Sheer and Michael Vachon were as helpful as ever with the entire project. The responsibility for the text is, of course, entirely mine.

About the Author

Joyce George

George Soros is chairman of Soros Fund Management and is the founder of a global network of foundations dedicated to supporting open societies. He is the author of several best-selling books, including *The Bubble of American Supremacy*, *Underwriting Democracy*, and *The Age of Fallibility*. He was born in Budapest and lives in New York City.

PUBLICAFFAIRS is a publishing house founded in 1997. It is a tribute to the standards, values, and flair of three persons who have served as mentors to countless reporters, writers, editors, and book people of all kinds, including me.

I. F. STONE, proprietor of *I. F. Stone's Weekly*, combined a commitment to the First Amendment with entrepreneurial zeal and reporting skill and became one of the great independent journalists in American history. At the age of eighty, Izzy published *The Trial of Socrates*, which was a national bestseller. He wrote the book after he taught himself ancient Greek.

BENJAMIN C. BRADLEE was for nearly thirty years the charismatic editorial leader of *The Washington Post*. It was Ben who gave the *Post* the range and courage to pursue such historic issues as Watergate. He supported his reporters with a tenacity that made them fearless, and it is no accident that so many became authors of influential, best-selling books.

ROBERT L. BERNSTEIN, the chief executive of Random House for more than a quarter century, guided one of the nation's premier publishing houses. Bob was personally responsible for many books of political dissent and argument that challenged tyranny around the globe. He is also the founder and was the longtime chair of Human Rights Watch, one of the most respected human rights organizations in the world.

· · ·

For fifty years, the banner of Public Affairs Press was carried by its owner Morris B. Schnapper, who published Gandhi, Nasser, Toynbee, Truman, and about 1,500 other authors. In 1983 Schnapper was described by *The Washington Post* as "a redoubtable gadfly." His legacy will endure in the books to come.

Peter Osnos, *Founder and Editor-at-Large*